By the same Author...

Society Awaken - Book 1
Society Doesn't Include Disability Fairly

Society Awaken - Book 2
Millions of Us Have Yet to Awaken to the Destruction of an Easy Thing Such as Drink/Drug-Driving

Drunk Driver Under the Light
A life of excursion

Drive Your Life a Mystical Adventure
Some admiration some distrust denials and detriments

The Simple Things

Podcast
Life taught social lessons in growth,
denial, accepting and learning

YouTube Jd Rodriguez
@jdrodriguez-ne4qr

...life lessons from a survivor

Denial, Dignity and Deviance

DRIVEN REALITIES - A PSYCHOLOGICAL VOYAGE

BY JIM RODRIGUEZ

This edition first published in paperback by
Michael Terence Publishing in 2023
www.mtp.agency

Copyright © 2023 Jim Rodriguez

Jim Rodriguez has asserted the right to be identified as
the author of this work in accordance with the
Copyright, Designs and Patents Act 1988

ISBN 9781800945463

No part of this publication may be reproduced, stored
in a retrieval system, or transmitted, in any form or
by any means, electronic, mechanical, photocopying,
recording or otherwise, without the prior
permission of the publisher

Front Cover Image
Copyright © Jim Rodriguez

Cover design
Copyright © 2023 Michael Terence Publishing

Contents

How To Get Kids To Listen 1
Mental 4
Preview 7
A Wealth of Experience 18
Creating Your Existence 25
I Have A Dream 30
My theory 32
An Incomplete Taste For My Intention............................... 34
Unapparent Nonsense Into Obvious Truth 59
Identity and freedom of will... 61
Correspondence: Is Reality Real? 63
Greed and Fear... 66
Concepts... 68
Why Is Drink-Driving Still An Issue? 73
Humanity 76
This Plan Is Apt 78
Acceptance 79
Behaviours Are Reinforced 80
Communicate 81
Memories.. 83
Spiritual Emphasis 84
Remember This.. 92
Implanting Lessons 93
To Our Future 95
Still Have Faith 97
Bibliography... 98

How To Get Kids To Listen

I will not truly appreciate parenting until I have kids myself, yes, I have heard parenting is a difficult job, but do I really acknowledge, all the nuances? Mealtimes, bath times, illness, and doctor visits, assisting homework, emotional unrest. The list is endless, I think I only consider giving a kid a good foundation and the lessons a difficult life allowed me to learn that I would teach.

I would acknowledge difficulties with a naming word to recognise their feelings, showing comprehension without questioning or giving advice. Kids like to get heard. At the same time nurturing using complex words used in context to add to their learning.

Denied feelings will infer a negative response, accepting and acknowledge their responses, will comfort.

Assist the child feel respected, listen, and accept with describing words. Decipher mere statements or moods with a child looking for empathy and explanation, don't just agree, get specific.

Good cures for anger in children: physical activity and drawing feelings. Let them show ya how they feel, sudden turnabouts from angry scribbling to drawing happy smiling faces is common.

Permit all feelings, just let them know boundaries. Tired, busy parents can greatly upset children, easily resolved; just presence is sometimes enough.

Expression is just as important as words, let them feel what you're saying, and don't over emphasize or agree with self-directed name calling. Acknowledging with just a word of calming reply can often lead to self-directed problem solving. Describe their feelings, they feel accepted, this is often enough.

Give them reason and a new way of looking at situations. Don't push bad feelings away, this will lead to worse reaction. Don't argue a fact, even if wrong or defeatist, agree with and grant in fantasy.

Stating the obvious can be enormously comforting, let them know ya know what they are going through.

Real listening is hard work. Reassure them and repeat real intention. Do not insist on do's and don'ts, implant true comprehension, enhance a climate of true co-operation.

Put into perspective and always remember, praise is vital.

Reference:

How To Talk So Kids Will Listen. And Listen So Kids Will Talk, Adele Faber and Elaine Mazlish.

Children do not do what parents say, they do as the parent does.

Do not get me wrong, I had a very good childhood, just my awareness now I have grown, tells me my past errors in judgements, were partly due to lack of real knowledge inclusion in my teaching, and a reluctancy or imposition when I was a teen for reason of making a tough time and life at home more enduring.

Now I have in mind knowledge of what I would not hide or portray to a child, and what I would demonstrate. I know this is all good saying this stuff but equally other parents can look at themselves, compare notes and makes adjustments. I am aware parenting is not easy, but there are some quite regular scripts of life, that I feel missing from my youth, and I was allowed too much free rein. I love my mother very much but self-doubt urges on critical thought about how things could have been better.

This annoys me that my parents are non-accepting of my views, argue with most statements and feel they did adequately.

I would sit with a kid, even teens and talk wholistically and inclusively, all with a mind of how they are growing and how they view their world. Even about what I might not like to admit affects them. Including strategies of coping and ways of looking at everything. Utilizing metaphors to demonstrate actuality.

Don't talk simplistically, use descriptive feeling words to invoke emotional response, not denial, repression or submission. This is in part how psychology worked in rehab, he would try to get a reaction with everything, this told him a lot about me and if the wrong reaction was made, he would teach the correct response.

Discontent leads to becoming distant, from others and objective reality. I am talking from personally felt times.

The most affecting disagreements do not have to attain a major topic, the little effect of this becoming so is what ya can call major.

Acknowledge and consider, I really would not mask feelings, these hidden agendas teach the child more than the lesson imparts. Don't think these agendas go unsensed, possibly the child will not have comprehension, so confusion ensues and the child is, unintentionally possibly, misled. Remain open about feelings and assumption. Don't deny feelings, open a dialogue.

References:

Behaviour In Public Places, Erving Goffman.

The Book You Wish Your Parents Had Read (And Your Children Will Be Glad That You Did), Philippa Perry.

Mental

Where science or society interacts with the good life, there becomes complications, facts, figures, tests or jealousy, secrecy, or deception. Other complications that have affected personally: patronyms, self-gain, trickery. Yes, from even the awakened!

I was diagnosed with mental illness after a severe car crash, though they could not locate a definitive diagnosis. That is because this is in part contributed to the Divine revealing, mixed agendas, ulterior motives, programs of belief programming my programmable future, and intoxicants.

To approach an experience without a sensibility about the intention is a missed opportunity.

Thought I knew the intention, am still following that hunch, but I had too many questions, of other morals, of my own obligation and right, of a real world. I have many. Firstly, I had unfair disadvantage in preparations, then I was programmed with inaccurate sub-conscious thoughts and beliefs that I did recall when due to. This is why I respect our minds like never before. I was in tune to the unseen by many little giveaway tones that revealed more than words, and fear was constant.

This was generating missed wisdom. I had to gain other directives to the narrow gate. So, I research reality and mind and thought, I deliberately reprogrammed my false beliefs and programmed a new intention and a different destiny than these false informative gave me.

People with disabilities are wise to uneducated burden, I did not ask for more burden, but this makes me stronger. Do ya want to check if I am bragging? Do ya want this wisdom? Then go on, live on the edge and ya can confirm all my warnings.

Do a reality jump back to sense, otherwise dive the abyss.

Ya will then learn of services ya once thought was for behind closed doors and only for the needy. Do not be dissatisfied with your lot, dealing with twenty years of scrupulousness is a lot not to remain content with. Do ya want to compare?

Think ya have a difficult time, I show ya difficulty, here have a drink!

Swagger

Girls are good with numbers, boys are better at football, these are unconscious biases that are inbred. The gender or disability bias are developed from a young age, disillusioned parents are teaching their kids how to get biased.

Unconscious bias does not explain all prejudice or discrimination, disability bias is largely unexplained, as an assumed predisposition.

People are offering prejudice whether they are trying to use the person with a disability, which some do, I offer personal experience. Or they are feeling sorry for us. They are discriminating in a not totally negative way but when they find out ya were a drink-driver, their pity alters to an attack, verifying that this was your own fault. They often totally alter attitudes and their tone changes, suddenly they become more in line with the desired non-judgemental person we wish all could remain, but what happened? I am still the same person ya pitied or thought pathetic 2 minutes ago, now ya getting verbally aggressive! So demeaner alter in the blink of an eye for some, why can these some not comprehend mood swings after a person's neurology was bashed? They seem to lose all responsibility for empathy or connection.

Many biases develop through societal and parental conditioning and are held at the sub-conscious level, they are unconscious beliefs. Comedians make use of these unconscious beliefs to deliver a punchline, they are so common. People get the joke but will not admit to having a bias.

Left-handed dominance has been discriminated for years, think of scissors or cameras.

We are all bias, we cannot avoid this, because bias is implicit. This is good to become aware of our own biases and really get to know ourselves and how unconsciously influenced we are by social-media, adverts, news, society and media.

Instincts and first impressions are important, often utilized by professionals. Parental instinct tells a parent when something is wrong, when professionals get their first impression wrong, they may think they are dealing with an over reactive parent.

Mothers and girls are less likely to get listened to by the medical profession, studies have shown. This is bias.

Context and cognition work together, to comprehend human behaviour we must look at the environment, context, and the mind, cognition. This is why there is such scope between cultures.

Conformity defines our world; this affects what we choose to remember. Conformity can become harmful, conforming to all the impressions ya received throughout life, leads to, my example, children possibly thinking ya do not make eye contact with a person with a disability, do not stare! Sure enough even some adult retort to thinking this is politically correct. A in some sectors, this has become a social norm.

Conformity is compliance with identification that has been internalised.

Whether we are in public or socialising at a private venue, this determines bias. I have found I am treated differently by the same people when in different scenarios. Whether or not other people are watching has one of the biggest effects on relations, this is proven in tests.

A norm is the rule of thumb, the action/reaction rule: other people react different- macro, or a person acts in the best possible way- micro.

Preview

What I once thought supernatural, has taken years to evolve to prominence, this rules my life now. Nothing is or can get hidden from the universe, careful just what unjust actions ya carry out.

Disability is more personally enduring than just the visible if any physical affects. A deduction in confidence enhances brain to redeem overpowering control over my chosen functions, I was unknowingly in survival mode because of the social barriers I put up with every day, from an *understanding* society.

Passionate about inspiring others.

There has been a light switch just out of reach but glowing brightly, with me my entire life. One day this light was switched on but my stubbornness stopped the most getting made from this light. Here is what suffering my youth, naivety and denials taught me and approaches I learn in my adult life. I never, before the last ten years did, or even appreciate and utilize the things I was good at.

If ya have talent or are skilled at something, make a hobby out of something then seriously consider that this can forward your career, or at minimal earn ya some money.

Started driving, do I need tell ya what the drinker did?

Crashed my car, five months hospital not including most of a decade of interspersed living between mental-health units and hospitals.

Ya may become proficient in any area after viewing occurrence from multiple perspectives/sides. Not just in mentioned but the tangible too, personal relations, deeds, emotive qualities and all the other unseen traits of life.

Man is the produce of his/her life script, the social world is the product, and has a dialogue. Not so much in isolation but collectively the two interact with one another. The product therefor acts back on the producer.

The secrets revealed in this book should be objective and taken seriously, they will improve lives greatly.

What just my aura, without words is teaching; anti-drunk-driving, we all say we don't, but the figures say lots of us do, why we don't get this yet I do know, because the lessons are taught all wrong. Everyone lives with survival instinct pressuring their ways and decisions, a massive, hidden to a lot instinct, is self-preservation.

Make your lesson visual, the poster on the train does not do much, so add auditory. And take something dear away from them, paint a picture they visualise having lost so something. So: hobble back and forth; visual. Shout really loud; audible. Take something away in their imagination.

Pass the feeling, silence the room.

Will cause people to think not only of not drink-driving, but the entirety of the rest of their lives.

Start From Where You're At

In the construction of social reality, John R Searle asks the question how is there a reality independent from us? I thought lots about this statement, to start with, I thought there so is one independent from us but when I considered all my past action and thought and how my evolution was turning out, I realised my todays were made by my very own or other people's influences.

He also asks how the various parts of a world relate to one another. A topic of my covered in other works. Was advised years ago to think best and that we create our own futures. Did not take this seriously, so again I learned the difficult way.

Hard work is not a smooth sound and is recommended not to utilize, but these times were nothing else.

I once wrote, because I witnessed this said somewhere, take the arduous path for more satisfaction when ya arrive at completion. Going through the narrow gate is a difficult place to find but leads to more satisfaction, this is the recommended gate to enter, entering by the broad gate, which most do, only leads to destruction. This gate is easier to find but more difficulty ensues.

How am I responsible for this non-independent reality? Still have argument to follow but simply because I did not do what top actors, sports and business professionals practice, that is to own yourself, keeping hold of productive words, never uttering a bad word about yourself or others.

I have had my esquires, do not plan to go back; unless time travel to an exact place in my past, retaining all I have learned since and all memories, retaining my abilities and regaining what I lost is possible.

In my other works ya learn huge amounts about your views, society, disability, conditioning, mind and more, all with the anti-drink-drive message attached.

Anyway, back to my history, affecting today, a fact some cannot comprehend but this is factual. This happened because of myself, by others advise and the bigger picture having affect, ya can say; that's obvious, how this works for everyone.

Yes, I muttered some untrue and unwholesome words, some were simply by text message. These were the first to show, they, most of them came to resemble my truth, a truth that is far from really who I always was, the opposite in fact.

Never talk, think, write, or text about yourself or others negatively, unless ya want repercussions. Energy is a big factor here, some may consciously or unconsciously sense the negative impression or just feel negative vibes and this can affect your next interaction or even that persons day. Put out negative this shall return, so put out nothing but good, this shall return.

Never procrastinate or ruminate on less good times or they only get worse.

Social

Like a person who boasts a macho demeanour may look over his shoulder to check no one is looking when he walks into a library, a person with a disability has this heightened awareness everywhere, even added socially stimulating increases in anxiety will include this awareness when in private.

I matured with awareness for various reasons, although this is bothersome this can lead to some very social aptitudes; astuteness, empathy, alertness to name a few. Though I am sure there are less drama-based ways to train the mind, although I believe natural selection and instinctive behaviour will surpass magnitude of purely training unless done with dedication.

My interpretation: The less understood the lack of similarity, the less people are keen to get to know ya. Personality factors determine this also.

Not many truly comprehend just how much a head-injury can affect. Emotionally, personality, judgements, thoughts and senses as well as physically. Also, comprehension of all of the above having dramatic deviations in affect and that can change with years and familiarity.

Man's conscious has a basis in sociology. Unless ya have reason to not realize equal citizenship, ya may not have the ability to appreciate the struggles of just facing an *all understanding* society. Some people comprehension and people skills are lacking when either deficit wants to acquaint new people.

Example: a disabled young man drove his scooter to town on a weekend night, parked and unfamiliar with societal reaction, he confidently went to mingle, he was immediately shut down in every interaction.

Avoidance

There are many differing types of avoidance. A most harmful one is uneasiness about certain issues a person may have. This can do the sufferer long-term damage and harden beliefs in the administered.

There are many different disabilities, the girl born without a nose who writes a sentimental letter to lonely-hearts will have quite a different experience than the man who walks unique/unusual. Yes, and even invisible disabilities are avoided.

Relative worldviews are altered every day by those avoiding and they will not know any better.

The ideology that a lot of us are encouraged to dream about is only a segment of a potential opponent's thought. Why does this affect so many? Because this is quite a character determining piece of the puzzle. Do these people even consider what I consider equal treatment? Yes, my ideal is most probably an everyday, long-term occurrence for them, but they fail to inherit or readjust their subtleties.

Is true, what we are familiar with, we take for granted, we are conditioned to behave inelegantly when about people with an abnormality.

Class interests seem little differentiated when this comes to attitudes. Yes, ya get advantage takers to over sympathisers to people who assume they are superior to a few, that consider all have rights, and all distortions throughout.

Disabled ideology is not met by many classes, but is anyone's? Everyone in society participates in reality-knowledge, some are aware of some of another's knowledge, some are not. We can never know of all other people's knowledge, and they can never know all yours.

Disability I say is a most difficult lived experience and behaviour in others I think is just unfamiliarity. Knowledge is lacking and even getting close to the store of a disabled person's knowledge is, I don't like to utilize this word but one of the impossibilities of life. Why I say you're looking beyond the impossible, this writing delves my knowledge but even this does not capture more than an essence.

Integrated thought largely determines treatment toward a person with a disability, also equally deciding the response. Because of the belly ache of familiarity, anger may get shown but survival again, will fight against the reaction to display the refusal to acknowledge.

The dual nature of society, in terms of objective facts and subjective meaning, makes each of our realities. How do subjective meanings become objective facts? In so far as to say how does someone not taken seriously, become someone who is really alive?

Knowledge guides conduct of all people in everyday life, the amount depends on how that knowledge is acquired and what is done with this. I am reminded of a saying which is, just because ya have arrived does not imply ya have gotten there, what will ya do while ya there and who will ya remember and who will remember ya.

How many can ya affect with your story? People with a disability all have their variations, like anyone, give us chance, yes possibly extra patience or comprehension may in some instances be required, certainly not in every case though. Ya can definitely broaden your horizons and will most likely learn a thing or two.

Remember

Serious car crash, splinter, or emotional unrest, whatever the size trauma, remembering the event is how phobias are made. Remembering causes distortions, so maybe, most probably the event is not recalled accurately. Trauma- remembering- phobia. I think fear, certainly for my definition, fits into this.

Most people do not like to face discomfort, in themselves or others. So viewing a disabled person not only reminds them of their own mortality but also reminds them of their own scrapes and near misses. This brings these instances more real to them, the mind does not like to take risks so this will present discomfort.

So, let us expand, my definition of disability prejudice: People view me lurching along- this makes them uncomfortable, perhaps adding fear assuming I am drunk, and unpredictability goes with drunks and, I state here, only some people with physical disabilities. Those injuries or illnesses that only affect physical appearances, don't necessarily intend volatile or unstable reactions.

Social tediousness can cause reluctance, no patience or anger in a few people. Yes some have amazing resilience and are not affected but so commonplace is angst between our feeling treated equal and social impositions.

Tempting to predict anothers internal dialogue, which no one can warrants my defence.

They do not know how to behave, perhaps they realize just how soul destroying an affliction can be- discomfort. I state here that these are not necessarily bad people, some have empathy, some others feel lucky to not suffer similar, some are curious. Bad people are those who immediately view an opportunity for advantage taking in a negative way. How can this possibly be in a good way ya ask? Example: a mother stopped me and said, I am educating my child, will ya explain what is wrong with ya? I just want to show her disabled people are still normal, all have a story, and this is usually ok if they approach. So she was taking advantage of meeting a person with a disability for a good reason. But I will also add, she was teaching her child wrong when she delivered micro-aggressions and spoke in a demeaning tone and ask pathetic questions, even for a child's comprehension. So she was displaying a form of most the above, the child will then sense her fear, this teaches the child more than the lesson did.

Now ya get every level of person from the questioned to the questioner, and every reason. Some naïve and patronizing, others with no feelings and take advantage to them that have sentiment and find work in the caring realm, though ya hear horror stories.

We all modify our experience of the world by what we think, feel, do, hear, or view. We pay attention to what we are doing, have done, or plan to do. All positions are influenced, some are phobia inducing, other times enriched by outside matters.

Keep control of what factors hit your internal triggers and stay strong enough to not totally allow a determinism of sway to negative affect.

Master life making. More reward for yourself- when the mind senses reward, serotonin is released, but also better for others, your mind will sense reward. More release of the feel-good chemical, ya really don't require drugs or alcohol to feel good!

Think, feel, do, and pay attention, there are zones of this model that are not accessible to all, they most probably have no interest in bettering themselves, or some will even find manipulative reason to excuse.

The worlds of seeming other realms or far off lands are seen as less urgent, disability was unimportant to me before my accident, because I thought this a hard place to get to when this is very, very, very easy!

Disability remained a secluded far-off land, when I found myself included, my reality, knowledge, and skills all changed, I was faced with surrealism and they all required constant work and awareness, in this secret world I found myself in. Secret because no one is fully aware of this construction and province of meaning, until ya qualify as impaired, then there is no tutor to educate the surreal, then there are levels of comprehension and differing magnitudes. The instincts rule now and over-power most self-directed decision ya made freely at one time.

People must reorient and attempt to find themselves the most suitably adjusted temporal structure of everyday life. Urged on by not giving in with what their live's challenge them with.

Life is shared with others, but mutual feelings of respect and other morals are not always. A general distaste for impairment in truth is general disregard in some instances. I am talking from memory of my very bad ability days, I do not intend to moan, I am simply making aware for those people who live with severe impairment, and educate the community who do, without knowing, often cause damage.

Society is subjective/not literal and not so much objective/real. The social stock of knowledge is taken for granted but sometimes, is actually false, less popular stock, is common between impaired people but assumed subjective.

Conformity is compliance with identification that has been internalised. Whether we are in public or private can determine our biases. Often we are treat differently by the same people in different scenarios. If other people are watching affects this.

Thoughts are either implicit- unconscious, or explicit- more controlled conscious. I would add here, or divinely orchestrated.

The aversion to any kind of danger is an internal process.

Tests have shown that just darkness can influence participant responses in experiments.

Heuristics: we go for what is familiar or recognised. Adaption is possible, unconsciously; we will go with the safe option of aversion from discomfort.

Consequences: making a person more alert to slight threat even if not really present, hence why darkness affects.

Ostracization: the act of ignoring or excluding those with differences.

People must choose the best, interpreted course of causal reaction. Affected by many phenomena, mental and actual.

We are more likely to exclude a person in the outgroup.

Marginalization: the presence of a trait that is a deviation from the norm.

Stigma toward a person/group or thing is a social construct. Disabilities affecting the person in questions psychology negatively is a social construct, not a medical model.

References:

The Construction of Social Reality, John R Searle.

The Social Construction of Reality, Peter L Berger and Thomas Luckman.

Recovery and Mental Health, David Pilgrim and Thomas Luckman.

Sway, Pragya Agarwal.

A Wealth of Experience

Experiences first taken as hard and unfair led to a life full of important lessons later regarded much. Is only in hindsight that I value the tough times I had to bring me to the person I am today. My work, seeming part memoir, that is because there are things to learn from my whole life. I wish I was taught exactly what my life has shown me, I feel obliged to teach these very lessons, ya can learn much from devastation. Do ya wish for a similar life or will ya learn from my time?

Always felt I wanted to educate others on important life lesson but severely underestimated myself. Life has told me that I know vital things if ya want to succeed at existence, or even lead an ordinary productive life. By ordinary, I intend to teach things magnificent, but maybe ya happy with a plain productive life, with nothing from the ordinary, how about knowledge that can transmute the ordinary to extra.

Thought a calm first 20 years was to continue, unemployment, study, searching unsuccessfully in all the wrong places and few friends since school age, moved home the year I left school, life got quieter and more silent.

From driving his life in the wrong lane, to conquering a self he never knew.

Visual mind.

Ever knew.

Childhood was an absolute fairy tale, climbed trees and made dens, united the whole school to a mass game of football and won every race on sports day. Lived with Mum and Sis, even when a man moved in, he never realised but he needed a proper

Father figure to teach him vital lessons of growth. Instead, he learned about emotions and facades. Learned all his life the difficult way.

I shall stop myself there.

Considering less fortunate people I have had an acceptable life, there is always someone worse off, lives would not resemble if we did not experience the good and the best- am learning, never to utter a less than opposite.

This continued into adolescence but he thought the lessons and trials were meant to get easier, instead was the hardest deviations to date.

He once had friends to share his time with, he should have regarded these more and cherish memory as life was to get lonely. He had an impeccable visual mind, and astonishing imagination, could visualize anything and he did, this made him feel with might that his life was profound, but he figured he was nothing special, having had all his talents played down, and although this is important to let kids have fantasies, they were awash with normalcy as one catastrophe was attempted to get hidden.

His visual mind he later learned was no coincidence. He was to adopt the power of visualizing for healing, this is so powerful, more than he inclined.

Did not feel comfortable anywhere, but he ignored anxiety, his mind would keep him company and occupy him, from an early age he did not realize but his subjective reality was largely in the mind. He too was to unfold this truth in decades time.

He has heard this best not to live in the past, does not have a wealth of good memories anyway. He was so caught up in his wonderful colourful mind, most of life slipped by without notice. He just remembers the poor events; a negative memory is recalled easier and before a good memory. So, this being how so, is best he does not transport back there.

Imagination can and will take ya anywhere, the mind does not distinguish between an imagination and a real event. Your conscious input tells ya your imagining but the second of our dual minds operate without conscious directing.

He wishes with his shoulders, that he was encouraged more to appreciation of hidden motive, I learned most what I know from living amongst and working out impressions. Also invisible qualities, independence and other foundations of adulthood, and given more responsibilities. Serious conversation was replaced with little belief and expectation, he figures he would be more today if more was expected from even the kid in him. Afterall what a kid learns, stays with them, treat a kid like a child and they will meld into your desire. He did not have social parents, this affects the child's growth too.

Think of childhood like a building site, for the tallest buildings to stand strong they need the best foundations, offer a kid few foundations, they will continue to fall.

A want to express has always laid, as a fairly non-expressive character he has though got knowledge to share. Wisdom grew in his years, something bound after treachery. He faced challenges after his fib of a fantasy childhood, he began by not comprehending, he was still in false fantasy, never having been snapped out of this when I demonstrated taking this feeling too far, he was therefor certain of his destiny. How did this appear, but that was not to be the worst.

He is a middle-aged adult now, having badly sown seeds, he reaped a scarce harvest. Eventually he recalls the diamond seeds he had sown long ago and continues by making these prominent in mind, so they affect change.

Mind travels, purpose uncovered

He floated through his early time oblivious to life determining dogma, he really struggled when he required mature wisdom, but this was growing, a multi-faceted form of alternative wisdom.

Badly sown seeds caused a reason to commit to searching for answers, this also led him to having to really concentrate on who he was and what he was about, and this results in purpose unveiling. He became the architect of his own identity as he was unfortunately identified by disability, after never growing up rightfully, he immaturely, severely injured himself.

He had a drink-drive car crash when 21, the introduction to adulthood was mangled. Because of his limited streamlined learning, and other tremendously affecting, character warping incidents or baggage, this was an extra test on his durability.

He met with obstacles like he only had nightmare about, the crash became obsolete and not the most determining. Adjusting to the resulting humanity was duress. He learned proper appreciation and finally regarded his mind, although this was now tarnished. He use mindful agility the best he can, never did he utilize this until devastation inferred; use or lose, and he lost.

This brought him to appreciation, he went on a self-made mission and discovered that a vibrant mind is nice but certainly not necessary for a happy, productive, and creative life.

On he goes, alongside essences and advantages, solitude, and stigma, he turns all his quiet time into writing and recording. His life will not be worthless, helping him develop into a life educator. He began talks on disability and anti-drink-driving, carefully using the previous to defer. This was very successful, he once proclaimed defeat but he found strength and rebuilt himself through self-healing. He remembers affecting alterations in road safety enforcement courses and is happy with his accomplishments.

Diamond seeds

He along with vivid mind, dreamt dreams that create worlds. He has a vision to alter the figures for drink-driving. They, after not budging huge amounts for years, have dropped nearly by half in the last 20 years. Now is that synchronicity or did my words have the great affect I was hoping? My first talk; 20 years ago!

Virtually honour a life, because my life allows me to give ya sublime teachings. There is no reason why ya cannot make best better and get this, live by this knowledge up front.

I dream today of how life would have evolved if I knew this stuff punctually.

Began life

Lacked substance, life skills education and full of a sort of naïve self-importance. Was a dreamer but not ambitious dreams just childlike daydreams.

Something kept telling me life's going to get good. This was the Divine talking, which I did not regard; higher power guiding my thought.

Feel like I am three quarters up that staircase, after travelling many journeys up many paths. With losses and continued opposition, which I am strong enough to have victory over. Do not ever doubt yourself or believe in fanciful horror stories. Create your desires.

I am adept at this advice for one main reason, ya live through an experience and ya become proficient, even expert, but living and advising are each end of a spectrum, I can advise better than practice but the practice of altering fate, I am very good at.

Lived life

In disregard, little gratitude and no belief, in the early quarter of life anyway. I just kept asking with my mighty mind, why am I so lucky to get all this, something will come from this, I did not know what.

Failed to grow up in my prior reality, so was forced to in a beginning twisted one. Reached Divinity, but through my own words warped my reality again, then I had to diverge back onto my amazing path and continued with effort to reach the enlightening experiences of this sacred planet. I am still trying.

Careful how and what ya speak, think, write or imagine. Only do these in good ways to allow your best to emerge, and this will.

Find myself here, drunk-driving nearly killed me but has since given me the most rewarding experiences of my life. Talking to large audiences, as a person who considered himself as a bit intimidated, making definite difference in the attitudes, thoughts and actions of others for the best. Witnessing not only children learning but adults also, not just witnessing but creating that masterful learning environment.

Realizations always known but taken for granted

Am starting from where I am at today, this has been a mighty journey, but I started to realize and try my best.

Am often talking about my life long ago when I present knowledge of what is waiting at the edge of drink-driving. Making aware helps people never to tempt such a one-way ticket. Can assist ya in sustain to not ever do this by drawing all your attention, with a few words, when ya do not want these in your experience, ya remember all I say;

Drunk driving is a direct path leading to either loss of identity because of injury, lack of acceptance after that injury because of debilitation, criminal record and/or fine, driving ban, loss of employment, prison, or perhaps your very own funeral.

If ya dare get in the car after the drivers had a drink, are ya tempting fate? Cause ya are, do ya not believe in probability and chance, odds are, ya will sacrifice through your own damn choice.

Many miracles brought me to today, did not believe in the correct things, so was shown a direction.

I am altering people's attitude for the benefit of everyone.

Do ya dream? Do ya daydream? Dream big, nothing puts a limit on the magnitude of desire. Remain careful though what ya imagine, this is a factor in your reality creation.

Learned so much because I made so many mistakes, but I continue and encourage the best, this is what I could have done from the start, do not get this near, get this right from now, today, and serenity is yours. I think is never too late to subdue your own mind. Though I have made the winding path more difficult, I will gain more when I traverse.

We all take differing routes but the staple is the same for each, think best, act best, believe best and achieve best.

May ya all have the best.

Creating Your Existence

Some suggested thoughts and statements to have and speak:

I know that God has fabulous blessings in store for me despite circumstances.

I have the wisdom of the Lord concerning every decision I make.

I am fully resourced to do everything God has called me to do.

I was born to rise above adversity and to triumph in the face of defeat.

Affirmations

I acknowledge my own self-worth.

I have the ability, support, and knowledge to achieve all the goals I set out to achieve.

There is nothing I cannot do.

I manifest great success, love, fulfilment, health, and creativity.

My self-worth is directly related to the success I experience and is increasing every day.

I acknowledge my talents and possibilities and am able to manifest them in this life to great effect.

I am good at what I do, I am.

I have many gifts to share with worlds and I share them openly and honestly.

I am a good friend and offer support and care to those I love.

My family, friends and partner, love and cherish me and I am fully deserving of their love.

Supported by Divine grace, I live in abundance.

I do not need to alter anything about myself to deserve love, success, and friendship.

I have the confidence to step out of my comfort zone so that I can learn and grow.

I am in control of my reality, and I choose to manifest good, happiness, and love.

I have all that I need to overcome life obstacles and live in abundance.

Living in light, I greet each day as a gift to enjoy fully.

Abiding in self-confidence, I share my talents and gifts with worlds.

I make a good difference in other people's lives.

I am respected, admired, cared for and loved, and I deserve all this.

My writing, thoughts and opinions are valued and well-received.

I am safe, supported, valued and loved, and this allows me to go through life with confidence.

I am inclined toward thinking of myself, although I consider my purpose, some say I do not often rebate myself. I truly believe is my duty to assist others.

Throughout life, my experiences, and mistakes, I talk of, so ya can all learn by me. Self-improvement, I apprehend we must all continue our development. Choose this, do not find a forced upon position of returning to fitness. If ya want a taste, the this is amenable, drink/drug-drive then or speeding in your vehicle can get ya here. Everything, and more that I mention can appear in your world, yes, just for yourself, this appears no one has similar experiences, and isolation, loneliness, disability and/or mental-wealth/health, differences in society, and friends and family, you're absolutely sure your going to risk living?

Do not talk of what I did because I want to wing, but because every word has something, whether obvious or not, consciously taken or not, has important lessons that sure enough get recorded by your subconscious and go on to remain and affect. All who listen to this, shall unconsciously alter negative beliefs or actions, and potentially add years to their lives.

Who chooses to listen will dramatically, as people in past have, alter their ways for the best. I am assuming people to take my intention and dismiss my errors; they take these onboard as they were made for everyone to learn by.

I am trying to redesign some of my past in others. I know what worked and what did not and effects of massive influence and perfect world statures, I am attempting to make everyone and everyone's world more perfect.

All can learn by my existence, judge me if ya feel inclined, but ya will learn and learn to teach others.

When I fail, I tell others. This is not my recommendation just I make use of all attributes to educate, one of my, and lots of people's biggest failings, some lucky enough continue until devastation, drink-driving. Walk, talk, think, dexterity is all much improved but some still issues. Do the same as me, who knows where this will take ya; better than, so ya continue, will catch ya in end. Worse than, I was affected extreme, but people have worse luck, paralysed or dead! Think of others if ya not going to think of yourself.

The people who know me have all learned from my life, just from close contact, they view or hear what I go or have gone through, and what I write. Most people that got whatever amount close to me since the accident, would not ever drink-drive or discriminate.

This book is an excellent gift, no matter their age, school, college, university, or work/colleagues. Mates or perhaps ya probably know drink-drivers, perhaps you're educating and nurturing, ya can educate adults. When they appreciate sentiment behind this action, they are eternally grateful.

I will stop any from drink/drug driving. Want a cure to drink/drug driving? This will work personal stories of disability, society and realities affect more than a criminal record.

There are many memoirs to show. Do not get fooled, these are not conceited self-fulfilments. I thought we would start with potential results of living these memoirs. All the while staying conscious of how easy ya can acquaint such qualified attributes and life skills after the wreckage that ruined or ended yours and/or other's/another's life.

Every excursion out was filled with horrors that society found acceptable. I hobbled to the traffic lights, two girls laughed loudly at me, then a teen who just passed me came rushing back, brushed past me simply to press a button for me; gee I can manage that. I carried on.

Further on the same journey a woman freaked at my staggering, perhaps she thought me drunk, and went over a busy main road. I carried on.

I stumbled, then stuttered a question, she turned away and gave the answer to someone else. I carried on.

I was exiting, about a hundred meters from door, a woman stood like a guard fully holding the exit open. I know she was trying to appease me but these actions insult some disabled people. Fair enough, hold the exit if we are about to go through, but for a whole minute, that is unnecessary. I carried on.

Very same exit, outside, I stumbled, still flustered, a man approached with a glutton look, got a cigarette? Lend us money, this is urgent? I carried on.

Can ya not envisage every time you're out, all this and more. This ya might find acceptable, perhaps ya even do some of these, well I am telling ya to stop. If the person is obviously going to have trouble exiting then wait as long as your life allows, do not assume before ya say anything. Do not become less courteous but do treat people equally. The disability rights movement has been misconstrued, people do not like to get enforced their manners, and people assume all disabled people are equal, they cannot make these equal to themselves.

Your subconscious is listening, so at the same time as mine hearing me say thankya for all the menial actions and think I must want this treatment, yours will record the prejudice, and changes are made, internally and externally, fact, this is science.

Good-intended folk harm as much as scroungers or ignorance, I know this is a hard swallowed statement, but I spoke about detriments on a massive psychological scale that micro-aggressions can have. Do not remain ignorant that you're doing the right thing, ya will know when assistance is required.

Can ya not put yourself in such situations? Disability prejudice has many faces and a lot think they are acting nice. I really hope I am educating.

I Have A Dream

Have dreams for worlds, dreams of what I am going to create in this life enabling enhancements to all civilizations. We do create our own existence. Create happenings and affect acquaintances and distant alike. By words, dreams, thoughts, even wild imaginings, we are creating.

Some of my imaginings, inferred by psychological neglect, have been overruled because my truth is known about.

What I call missability and spiritual-wealth, or lack of, both lead to great disturbances of self and society dealing with me.

People must learn to become thick skinned in a multitude of glitches. We lose much inhibition, sometimes this a good thing, other instances no.

I came from a very bad trauma, not much was in proper working order physically or mentally. I was reborn with much rehabilitation. Yes, physical ailments, no matter how bad they apparently are, can improve. I am still changing in mind and body 20 years later!

Most disabilities alter all social interaction, some more than others.

My ingrained stories

Kids would stare, scare, or laugh, kind gestures insult- I was assisted in pressing the lights button or a door was held wide open while I approached from 100meters away. Scroungers approach, in every town they sense a vulnerable streak. This is why a few people seem ignorant to anyone even present or why we may seem rude or out of character/order, so intolerable are some actions we must do something to sustain.

Walked in a place with someone who stood near entrance, I approached desk, near fell on way, got to secretary, ask question and unbelievably she swung on her chair and shouted answer to this person down the corridor!

Or a nice woman spoke to me in street, she said: alright duck, nice day, do ya come out often? Where's your Mum? Who looks after ya? Who does the housework and cooks?

Even people that I know ignore me, while their mate talks over sympathetically with me. Disability changes most of social interaction.

The subconscious, ruler of all, takes notes, and effects conscious decision. Ya will begin making choices/remarks ya always denied or even ones ya found disgusting and disagree with; showing gratitude for tedious petty courtesy, because you're polite! Your mind, in survival mode, now controls everything.

I had many a moment where I could not believe what I just did/said or thought. This ran totally against my belief system, I was ashamed.

Think you're strong? If ya ever regret drink/drug-driving or speeding, survival mode will make an appearance and your mind will lead and decide what is best.

Trust is a big word, ya do not have to believe me, just trust yourselves that life is good and staying that way; I would not drink/drug-drive or speed/reckless drive. Even if ya consider I am not speaking true or exaggerating. Life on the other side of an accident will give ya no choice but to learn all this and this has taken me over 20 years and I am still not familiar.

Or possibly ya die in the crash, cause heartache to loved ones, and they think and curse, why did they do that! Why did they not learn? We should have taught better.

My theory

Speak the truth and is more likely to teach knowledge gained. This textbook, worked through, is virtually guaranteed to affect/teach the unexpected norm in multiple areas.

I am very happy, I have had completed encyclopaedias waiting for their outlet, the moment has finally arrived. I wish to thank all entities that allowed creation and distribution of this work.

Largely biographical but when parts originated, memory was apparent. I pursue a universe of sense and inclusion, with deviance abolished.

The conceptualization is subjectively real, in as much as phenomena that to me seems saintly directed, the deviant concepts are spoken to expose those who think their intolerable gestures are secret.

With regrets I still portray learning from these concepts and show that, defining your reality is an ability.

Knowledge of treachery has value, to guard from. I have very direct knowledge of consequences and legitimizations.

You're all capable of finding a legit reason for opposing sense, manner, or regulation, to test the given rule, if ya like.

Regulate sensible manner and hindering regrets turn non-affecting and easy to avoid.

We are all deserving a landmark in evolution

I talk of what should, today, get taught in schools. I have mentioned emotional intelligence but also, the power of words/speech- on both parties, micro-aggressions, and reality creation/the power of all our minds, and disability inclusion, though I hasten to add, this has progressed since my day.

Do not comprehend the politics of even today's world, they portray trying to make worlds better places, so why is so much never revealed? Except to a few or them that afford such an education.

Most of society, or some of society cannot get ignored by selective selection. We must incorporate everyone.

I started out studying for continuing my own life rehabilitation, but I learned so much I felt I must share all this.

I have much to teach, and this book/podcast is a landmark.

This may start out trivial for ya but this material is assured to enrich yours and the people in your lives existence.

I have my own gripes about controversy, we do our best and are entitled to retort to controversy, the impact depends on your true want for the cause. I have a few, but improvements to overall humanity is top.

You're about to embark on the most affective and honest education you have received.

I learned massively, without grasping what I knew. Put into real practice, thou will witness life at another level!

This is part biography, my time was had to teach others, this life has much to offer those who seek.

Too much is withheld, I cannot grasp why and what sense this is, in a diverse place.

Regards, your author.

An Incomplete Taste For My Intention

Behaviours are reinforced, a negative reaction will mean the behaviour is less likely to be repeated, a positive response means the behaviour is more likely to be repeated. This is how we teach children but is just as true in adults.

Repetition and conditioning is how we learn and remember through behavioural psychology which is observable psychology, problem solving, remembering is cognitive psychology.

Person-centred approach involves what is going on surrounding the person.

Start where you are

Reviews for future book

This book is not only inspirational to myself but to my family and friends too. It has been riveting, eye-opening and brought out a wide range of questions to my daughters and myself. We have learned life values. J. Rodriguez is an inspiration whose story should be heard, I am proud to be his friend.

Book reviews

-This taught life-changing inspirational life lessons. Brought my family closer together and educated my parenting style.

-My 16-year-old was deterred from drinking and drugs.

-Has been a plus in all areas of our lives.

-You're definitely here for a reason, ya have a gift. Think you're on this planet to teach.

I am an honest person or is this laziness, but I have included exactly what I pre-empted and wrote which follows in both books. My Discoveries. Available at the Podcast (see the very first page of this book).

My writing has traversed to other places, I am starting from where I am at with 'My Discoveries' because I am sure you will benefit tremendously from these. Not saying that the book closes with any less important lessons but I wanted to get you as much value as possible early in, so you are enticed to turn the page. I have learned in my research, to make multiple little books rather than one big but the vision I have for this book entitles this should contain all my experiences. I am not greedy, offering value before seeking more profit comes first for me, stay with this book, you will learn so so much.

Times have altered much since I wrote the first fourth of this book and the narrative follows suit. I have been through realities differing for all fourths, this I am sure is apparent.

These early chapters are short, each on a single subject, well you may learn more than one trick on every page. I have began here because I am twenty years into a recovery, in my rehabilitation I had to relearn everything, is like reliving a life, I feel so lucky because I could overlay previous learning although they were vague now with new information. I became addicted to research; self-help of any kind and I uncovered some simple but helpful facts and remedies that anyone could use.

Friendship

An elemental need to belong. (*Friendship. The Evolution, Biology and Extraordinary Power of Life's Fundamental Bond.*, Lydia Denworth.)

I decided after a lull, to write about something extremely important to me but that which I am momentarily lacking, I write better when I have something of massive sentimentality to me. This moment has lasted far too long, I am lonely and remember all the pro-life things that friends allow to enter my life. I have met acquaintances who resist demonstrating the sublime attributes and deliverance that I am looking for. I know this is not exaggerated thinking, I have received all I ever wanted from mates before and have lived long enough to know true qualities when they are displayed.

The biggest reason I don't have friends is because I do have a disability, although many people say they don't hold any stigma, like this or not if you're not a person with a disability you don't know the truth, society tends to unconsciously underestimate people with disabilities so a lot will not even regard us as potential friends that can offer anything worthwhile. I also have a form of mental health and past intoxicated behaviour just confirmed people's false prejudices. I have so much to offer but only relax enough to reveal most of my real self when I am totally comfortable and connected and receive enough reciprocal vibes. This is truth: None of us truly gain total apprehension and importance of the necessity for life of friendship. Attachment is vital to some degree at all ages, there is a basic drive to connect. We fail to realize until we are walking in the shoes of experience, like disability no friends is an invisible soul destroyer.

There has been so many intense studies on childhood development, orphanages and childhood neglect point blank lead to deterioration, severe illness and complaints and death. Attachment is life giving, children need rightful love to flourish, basically this affects their whole life and physiology and how long a life is determined.

Relationships matter and are essential to life, you have got to learn how to love if you are to learn how to live. A unifying theory explains the behaviour of all species even stretches to humans. Enough humans have demonstrated this behaviour that this is known as human nature, evolution goes over the same relationship building in ants and primates. Altruism is major, some ants don't form social relations but dedicate their time to service. Reciprocal altruism is rewarded down to genetics which goes on to affect social behaviour. All human acts may ultimately be selfish.

In the first 1,000 days of life children have a preference for faces and voices, social communication starts early. Touch is the most developed sense in a newborn, a child who receives no intimacy or contact will sure enough have issues from emotional, biologically, neurological, social and health. Effective touch is a significant role, forging connections and increasing survival.

I had a very social attitude as an infant bringing together the whole school in a mass game of football and demonstrating other social aptitudes. Life changed at 7years old, this is the one of two only justifiable research driven reasons for my older issues in socialization, the other is a Spiritual reason, the third reason was created when I drank and drove to have a severe car crash, disability induced new realities in every realm, already troubled emotions, cognition and relations, disability encouraged a diffused society and perception of that scene. Environment and lifestyle and social integration or isolation determine physiology and health, fact. Any demand for change lead to stress, so these as well as social relations are connected to health because stress and social isolation are two of the biggest causes for mortality. Cigarettes and death, lack of social support both have a 2to1 connection to mortality. Social factors trigger differences in physiology, relationships alter physical responses to stress. Lack of social contact is the reason for my pathologies. Loneliness has cellularly connections to what is meant by, to be fully human. Mortality and depression are good arguments I can put to my social worker for extra support. Control and participation are crucial for health wellbeing and longevity that all follow a social gradient.

People who perceive high support show less cardiovascular aging. Everything psychological is biological. The social environment decides which genes are expressed, I am a very social person, meaning that I love to be in conversation with those I like. My support or isolation switches on or suppresses the expression and activation of the genome. I realise the sustenance I get from other people, This is enough to warrant extra support, I get that I need to get out more and I am growing toward that to increase my society but the support has got me on this path of increased belief in myself and confidence, I cannot forward a stronger disagreement for refusal of support based on her reasons.

A 75-year study says: THE ONLY THING THAT REALLY MATTERS IN LIFE ARE YOUR RELATIONSHIPS TO OTHER PEOPLE.

A TED talk with over 30 million views says: GOOD RELATIONSHIPS KEEP US HAPPIER AND HEALTHIER. SOCIAL CONNECTIONS ARE REALLY GOOD FOR US AND LONELINESS KILLS.

Learning

We learn by association, the bell was sounded every time the dog's dinner was put out, the dog continued to show with just the sound even when dinner was not accompanying. Learning is conditioning, if something happens often enough this is programmed or etched into the mind, physical or mental occurrence.

Association: We can associate good or bad things, we still learn. You learn to avoid the negative stuff when they are associated with less good abstracts.

Conditioning: affects people at a deep psychological level, disabled people all treated the same from society every day, makes us alter how we behave.

Children learn by imitation, as they are developing. Do not describe but demonstrate, this is a good theory for adults too.

Sensing adversity and suffering as chances for change and growth

Reference:

Learn Faster and Better, Josh Eyler.

Interview questions:

-ask questions to, learn, grow, connect, challenge, improve, develop

-I would like to know your perspectives. Whether you are able to envisage your evolution, example, I was under the distinct impression that I would never drink drive or have to live a solitary life with disability in tow, this was before I even began driving. Can you visualize how life changes from youth to adulthood and how what you so believed when younger may alter, until you are experiencing the life 5 or 10 or 20 years from now you cannot accurately claim what actions and thoughts you will make. life may have been difficult and unfair to ya, you might be in a situation where someone needs a lift, possibly it's just too cold or long a journey to walk, and late no public transport. can you really appreciate the future, I thought I could until I was in this future.

-how do you view drink drivers today? people with disabilities today? seriously you quite possibly will not think the same in years to come about anything, your experience and opinions change.

-why do we have these problems, how do we solve them, do ya think: I am not enough? i don't have enough? do ya want to think like this, because you will if ya have a brain-damaging, disabling car crash.

-what do you want to do with your lives? keep your personal control.

-what can we do to make a difference?

-what will ya do with the second half your life? don't end this in the first half.

-will ya trust me with your lives? if ya want to hold on to these don't drink and drive, make other lives better, be inclusive, don't judge, don't think all people with disabilities have done anything wrong.

Your Self Image

Y - yolk: you cannot have an egg without a yolk. Your image is whole when you behave complete.

O - organic: consume healthily and do not fill yourself with unnatural or harmful ingredients, drugs, alcohol, fat, chemicals.

U - ultimate: do not underestimate yourself if you sense somewhere, you are not behaving complete then fix this, get educated, experience, learn.

R - rich: you are as rich as you make yourself in emotional, personal, and sensual life, YOKE IS RICH AND HEALTHY ULTIMATELY LEADING TO A RICH WELLBEING.

S- signify: notify yourself consciously of areas you do well in and areas you are not happy with, work on improving all areas, you can get even better, there is an answer to everything, do not suffer.

E - enable: allow your learning, permit your talents to shine do not dwell on negative aspects of personality, concentrate on the good parts.

L - love: love others but save some self-love, demonstrate a kind heart and this will be reciprocated.

F - free: you are free to be as wonderful or as unhappy as you like. SIGNS ARE THIS IS FREE TO ALLOW LOVE TO ENTER AND FREEDOM IS YOURS.

I - imagine: never think negative words or images and especially do not talk of yourself or others in a bad way, be constructive if you have to.

M - manage: handle your mind, thoughts, actions, relationships, deeds, speech, attitudes.

A - age: you are as perfect as you tell yourself whether you are 10 or 100 years old. do not let others undermine this attitude, believe in yourself.

G - grant: you can give anyone anything, including yourself, use your imagination.

E - every: EVERYTIME YOU IMAGINE 'YOKE' YOU WILL MANAGE YOUR ATTITUDE AND AGE TO GET GRANTED A WISH OF YOUR CHOOSING.

-adjustment or atrophy, each day life and you are different adjust to change.

-go go or no no, stop blocking develop.

-enterprise or emptiness, get excited through your activities don't be bored and passive.

-accept, don't blame others or God, share with others, police yourself.

-forgive, forget the blunders of yesterday,

-who is the most successful person this century? Answer: you are when you fulfil yourself.

Respect

R - resurrect. revival after disuse inactivity or decay: revitalize your spirit when you feel the need.

E - eclipse, obscuring the light from one body by the presence of another: you can impose any identity over your old self.

S - suspend, state of expectation: anticipate only your best.

P - prioritize, precedence in rank: who is number one.

E - expect, regard as likely assume a future event: assume a good outcome.

C - confidence, firm trust feeling of reliance or certainty: trust your instincts.

T - treat, act or deal with a person a certain way: you are confident.

Psycho cybernetics, Maxwell Maltz. I got the suggestion of using acronyms from here, but they are created by myself.

Drunk driver.

I had a severe disabling drink drive car crash; I was unconscious for six weeks in a-coma at two points from brain death. I was not aware enough to enter back into normal life for years hence I was not charged. Please do not think that's not fair, I would rather the fine, the ban, the courts, the record than the twenty years of recovery since.

M. Palermo's audio documents very well the incidents of getting charged. I have documented his excellent story here because I lack experience in this area, I am very knowledgeable and written lots about disability, society, brain damage and altered realities.

Michael Palermo says in his audiobook he always gets this little sensation in his heart after visiting his daughters when he is on the way home. He was about to get a very empty feeling; he would not be able to visit them so often. He is lucky he is still conscious enough to recognize them. Lucky you say, he gets pulled by police, uh oh, he stopped for many drinks. He knows he is in trouble. His book is named diary of a drunk driver.

The start of a long process: He got in a wrestling match with a rough police trooper. The Breathalyzer was waiting after all the paperwork. He gets a ride home then waits twenty days to appear in court. He suffers the search for a lawyer, things are not good, he is over twice over the limit. He was lucky with the judge; he was let go until the trial but he had to surrender his license for a month. He has many very moving stories of what he witnessed in court and his life, he delivers a lot of observations. He continued drinking, during lots of walking and bus rides.

He gets a conditional license and constantly affirms he is not drinking and driving. Court: If he pleaded guilty, he would get three years probation, jail walk through, fifty hours community service, interlock device and a fine with counselling. (This is American).

He has other reasons to celebrate, he affirms he is not drinking and driving. He has disruptions with family, the sentencing date finally arrives, the judge likes him but he had not gone to the instructed counselling. So, he started twice a week for six months. They spoke in group sessions and one on one, in the group they spoke about whether they were ashamed, his answer was I made a mistake, they said we all make mistakes just try not make the same mistake again. The probation was a very busy time, he was put out for the whole probation period, I admire this man's audiobook, his story got even me thinking, he ends with sentimental deliberate statements about how it's not worth drink driving. I end with the two punishments, mine and his, are each troublesome in separate ways, so there are absolutely no benefits, no lenient punishment to drink drive… and ya could kill yourself or others. Think about this, I recommend his book I listened to most of this in one sitting and this kept me listening.

Thankya Michael Palermo

Cause to effect

If we participate in the cause then we have no choice but to participate in the effect. Bluntly stated in layman's terms: I participated in drink-driving, cause, so therefore it was not even a decision to participate in the 20 years of recovery, disability, social distortion, everything down to micro aggressions and expressions.

Live until you die, I died or rather my personality died. I had daydreamed about starting life over again with what I currently knew and learning more in a new consciousness. Be careful what you imagine, this is the best way I can explain exactly what took place. I had to relearn everything, consuming food and drink, walking, talking, emotional life, intelligence and learning. Was not until 20 years later that I fully appreciate the chance in devastation I have been given. Inspiration allows me to live again or rather for the first time. I was alive but never lived, narcissism told me I did but self-deceit is a trait. I am still not living a life many would be envious of but audio books, research and suggestion of studies have invigorated my soul, I feel alive more than I have in years and with desires and dreams for what I can do for others. Everything is slowly emerging, my long-awaited rejuvenation of returning to my talks, educating the masses and successful writing. I knew, I just knew this is occurring. Our lives are complete only when we allow and enter two massive areas of development. These processes are occasion and restraint. Use the occasion as fulfilling your chances whatever they may be and restraint to limit everything to reason, though do not underestimate your vision, restrain ego to control of environment. Utilize your energy wisely, let your inner authentic power and inner value glow.

Intention before action in this our great learning environment. I always had the intention even unconsciously to conscious intent to enhance the world- Intention. Has happened slow, my resulting action was to start public speaking, attempting to run a blog, webpage and message board, and write and publish books. I have one in publishing and have begun another with very different messages.

Effect

Follow and love intuition, let this guide cause and create effect. Do this with love.

I lost some power through an addiction I did not acknowledge to surpass; I was only temporarily stopped when this addiction along with addiction to felt invincibility lead to my world collapsing mind and body warping reality bending parallels became mine to exist in. I drank and drove into oblivion; addiction is not stronger than the soul, but I complete this balancing act without total healing. Is the magnitude greater than my desire, I do not think so, I can I have before defeated the odds, proved others wrong and beheld empowerment without total alignment. I choose my path and this all accumulates my lessons to substitute as healing parables. I work hard but do not impress myself until I refresh my mind by all my productions.

Wisdom says I do contain errors, but my personal choice does not contain much wisdom or perhaps there is good Divine reason for my inability to absolutely comply. I believe my intuition when this affects greatness of utopia, my anticipation of evolution is perfect.

Become a step away from yourself

Although this I only think is important to recognize and connect with your persona, I will talk of my success in detaching from an identity of disability.

Of course, this was nearly an impossibility, I still have not totally accomplished this. I have more so in attitude, but I do not consider my disability as a major debilitation, I was reborn with years of rehabilitation. This does not affect onlookers completely; they see me for the first time and witness lack of ability and confidence. Acknowledging strength and determination, or weakness and clumsiness depending on their style. This does not enter my mind to justify a judgement, they are on their path following their own intuition or behaving instinctively.

I found reassurance in disidentification, not a good psychologist, am I? Though this may not be a bad thing. Disidentifying with that that makes you feel vulnerable and in a minority group that owns little respect from the outside, is surely recommended. Collective human assumptions about disability made this a group I felt for but did not want an association to. During my research I witnessed many people with disabilities who are quite admirable people, I even fell for some recognizing their plight and their efforts to campaign. My experiences of and with severe brain damage meant most the people close to me had the same injury or illness, this means great irregularities of personalities, and including myself, back in the day we were all unable to deliver strong enhancements to disabled lives by teaching what we thought we knew to society.

This affected my ongoing view of my own group but have ambition to join some of these remarkable people I have viewed doing good work to promote disability awareness.

Reference:

The Seat of the Soul, Gary Zukav.

Death by a thousand cuts

I have found yet another passion that I will not only enhance my own humanness through but help make other lives less enduring.

My discovery of something known as micro aggressions, these are not conscious to all people although they are only well aware of the discomfort this cause, people suffering these micro aggressions every day or at least more frequently, report them having psychological effects on wellbeing. This runs deep and is a major cause of rift between the communities in all cultures.

So difficult to avoid not just receiving a micro aggression but tricky to stop administering these that I am intrigued, I know I am a culprit and resigned willingly to training and more research in this topic.

These so-called aggressions have become so regular conditioning has programmed me to think less about them, hence why I even stuggle to think of examples of the thousands of slights I have received. This is well known in the psychology of the human brain that any uncomfortable feeling is repressed and the more the occurrence the father this is pushed into recesses. I think this is why I am so enlightened by discovering micro aggression as a term, because we do not talk about them, do not even admit to aggression of any sort and are not even aware that a lot of people find what may be a mundane comment to you is deeply insulting to us.

When I am more relaxed with people, I am more likely to deliver a micro aggression, this is to say I, we can, should never totally drop our guard. This might be a hard comment to digest but is true if we want to continually appease and get along in society. The relaxed brain is not an efficient brain, its ease and inhibition of making mistakes is not even aware of itself, its societal common place ignorance is totally accepted even when these micro aggressions are talked about and explained along with the offence taken and are more often seen as overreaction and needless. I cannot sense much need for them and only attribute them to survival instinct, the body/brain knows of the trenches and how these, ongoing will cause neurotic scars so it is in protection mode.

The edifice and moral of the story is that we really can harm one another without the intention, no wonder then why there is corruption, not only are civilization causing harm to our neighbours unknowingly there are those that do this deliberately.

Deliberate to know as much as possible, do your research, listen to books. I find audio books easier, was getting through three a night in my discovery time, you can learn so much, and you will grow.

Unspoken agreements

The first thing I have to say is that, whether you are aware of them or not, silent agreements are contagiously rectifying and remain dangerous. They, without saying, with assumptions of sameness, can cause massive upset yet they are routine. Evolution has not taught us they cannot be relied on.

Yet have you ever said, 'that goes without saying'. Some agreements are just known but this is good to talk about your assuredness and the others likeness. I have found relationships of friend's flounder because of these unspoken mysteries.

Your sense of humility and connectedness probably is slightly off key. Not one will agree with absolutely everything and assumptions are not exactly accurate anyway. Relationships are difficult, communication has many facets, beliefs lead to other worlds, we live in an affluent, coinciding social setting. Life is the trickiest beauty.

Reference:
Avoiding conflict does not usually lead to peace,
M.L. Owens, S.R. Banks, L D. Anderson.

Silent agreements

Be honest and open about what you think and feel, not with everyone, discretion is recommended, only those closest should you totally trust and reveal yourself to. I am speaking from my experiences with trust, deceit and treachery. This does not have to be the way things are, talk, just talk openly. Open conversation is the saviour you are looking for.

Exclusion of awareness

This is my plight, which has very objecting actions displayed, to resemble the large portion of humanity. Larger than you may think or can appreciate but coming from a disability and mental health background experiencing both these in severe forms, I can as well as many others whose voices are just not listened to admit to colossal sectors of the community having too little awareness. No one or at least not everyone displays an unintentional behaviour to portray understanding but lack conscious awareness of their real effects. Have you ever offered a disabled person assistance with something you would find easy? Have you ever underestimated, talked down to unintentionally a person with a difference? This is what I am referring to, these actions cause bitterness, anger, useless feelings and isolation.

Even the most civil of society portray microaggressions that deeply affect the other. In Michael Barran and Tiffany Jana's book, Subtle Acts of Exclusion I learned that, apparently calling a person, possibly a black person, articulate is a micro aggression. What! I did not know that, can you comprehend the difficulty we all face trying our best, sometimes, to be inclusive and unoffensive. Paying our intended compliments but offending others.

Understanding and comprehending, critical feedback of another's experience will lead you to becoming a justified better person. Micro aggressions are in the most unintended but can affect just as much as deliberate racism or feminism or ableism. There is talk of documenting some microaggressions, this would lead to more comprehension of how innocent words can offend.

Some people will not even know what the term micro aggressions means, I will stop using the words discrimination, prejudice, and stigma because most of my disability experiences with society an unintended micro aggression or subtle act of exclusion are more common. Those who do not experience these regularly will fail to recognize the importance and affects and may presume innocence and over reaction. This is a major disruption in societies. I do not think anything of describing someone by physical factors, the black bloke, that disabled one, this is micro aggressions.

Assumptions, treating with less dignity and stereo typing, if you recognize you are displaying any of these, stop yourself and you will be opposing the chance of practicing unintended micro aggression. If people knew the harm, they may do I am in no doubt we would stop. Language I learnt is quite important the I learnt this is vitally important to community.

Conversation about our differences crucial. Maura Cullen, 35 Dumb Things Well-Intended People Say: She very rightfully says, you know the saying, sticks and stones will break my bones names will never hurt me ought to be sticks and stones will break my bones names will scar a lifetime. How people are affected by words and statements is only admirable to become aware of, diversity is massive and learning this, being inclusive will broaden your life. Also becoming educated on the lesser-known micro aggressions will make you a sublime individual, we have yards to travel as this word does not even enter most people vocabulary.

Over reaction, we overreact typically when we hear the same thing repeated so you can understand why people with disabilities get a reputation for seeming over reaction. Different deliverance of said unimportant comment becomes tedious. I have lost hope in many friendships because they totally validate their comments and dismiss my feelings. Now communication is just as vital, possibly I could have explained my frustration better, but brain damage affects at length and is particularly so difficult to understand it is not even understood enough to justify and explain. Privileged and disadvantaged groups typically have communication issues. If a person feels understood they are more likely to respond, just contemplate all the energy they have used repressing upsetting comments, intended or unintended. Sir Edmund Burke: The only thing for necessary for evil to triumph is for good people to do nothing. This is socially accepted by society when this comes to disability, being argued, or denied in society. I have experienced this, as giver and receiver, bystander behaviour needs courage to overcome.

Micro aggression offences

Some of my friends are, ... fill in the blank. I know exactly what you're going through... I do not think of you as... I get the same thing... I have personally felt these things said, they cause no admiration.

Diversity is about letting the person in question appear. Disability is not all the same.

Be conscious of making subtle acts of inclusion rather than exclusion and surely enough you will endow the detrimental behaviour that has no intent less and less, we all need this evolvement.

Unconscious bias

Everything you need to know about our hidden prejudices. Annie Burdick.

You like everyone else in the world has unconscious bias, this is unintentional and better than conscious bias, which is intentional, become consciously unbiased and recognize your thoughts.

The brain takes shortcuts and evolution has built bias that you are not aware of. Society influences our short cut seeking brains, based on what society has to say about any issue can trigger bias. Trauma can lead to deeply rooted bias which like all bias is combatted through recognition. Stereotype threat influences people in their own groups, social groups, religion, sexuality, ability, background, workplace. On public transport or in the street we all take part in active bias, describing someone by their gender or race. You can study bias for years and still relapse, this is normal is a part of the human condition, just don't let a bias unconscious or not, stereotyping or no don't let this active bias turn into action and this does not make you a bad person.

Acceptance, empathy and diversity are tremendously beneficial and educating. Citizenship and relationship status, mental health or illness, attractiveness is all possibly connected to disability making this a very common bias that the community find normal this is that unconscious. Social dominance, differences, religion, or beliefs all have huge bias but each with their own deviations in reason. Which makes bias an even more tricky subject that a lot are not even aware that they possess. Bias is so common this is found everywhere, even in health care and education. Both these go on to affect people with disabilities and people of different race or ethnicism who already have their own chains of bias. Institutional racism is even found in all aspects of the justice system over Europe other countries this is unheard of. When acknowledgement of disability bias becomes as mainstream as racial bias we will be progressing. People with a moderate disability are only 47% likely to get the job, I suppose that is fair being nearly half of all candidates but a severely disabled person this drops to just 25%.

Exploring your biases, you must have an open mind, get creative, get educated research, learn about yourself, practice self-awareness be mindful of your thoughts and focus on your instincts, have open conversations not only about your mission to uncover your biases with people you know. Then talk to others including those you do not know of different groups, talk about bias you may learn something, take an online test for implicit biases. This will uncover bias and help you become more consciously unbiased, remember to consider bias turned inward, do you underestimate yourself or think negative things about self. Take time to reflect and learn about yourself.

There are good and bad ways to talk about bias, react and talk about bias become an ally and speak up when you witness bias when the situation is safe, stand your ground but don't be aggressive.

As long as there is bias in the world there is reason to conquer bias. This journey is worth the effort and self-empowering. Question everything, reflect and add some love to the world.

Altruistic.

Friendship is dear alas essential for human life. My writing has taken priority over search for friends, but this work I don't agree is wholly altruistic because, no because nothing, no actually I do. I feel a great calling to complete this and really sense this having great effect on the globe. Morals help me stay on this path, not selfishness nor sympathy though I do feel sorrow as I have lived through my whole life and the past twenty years so know only too well the adversity of wrongful parenting well-meant or not and societal isolation and crippling aptitudes or actions, quite literally. Deviousness and trickery, disbelief and humiliation, chastity, and beliefs. Characteristics that follow my every move are reducing after years of sustenance. I was generalized and defined but wrongly.

Man, I hear is free to choose of his own free will whether so to ascend in the scale or descend. (Moral Powers: A study of Human Nature. Peter M Hacker). I disagree, my dignity was robbed and freewill became grace. Respect is due to all human beings; I feel truthfully respect was chastised. To destroy self-respect which is growing to replenish. As I feel remorse and repent my deeds and thoughts. This isolation, duty and loneliness is adequate punishment for late deliverance and unintentional shameful affecting, I shall deliver yet, ideology is virtuous after rationalization was made invisible. I have no capacity for wickedness but have befallen. Rationality is recognised as is extreme abnormalities and distortions. Conceptualizations considered I regard I have practiced detriments, due to unconscious retaliations of supernatural bad. Monstrous evil can happen to anyone in any society. There are many larger evils more common than my demon: The Holocaust and dozens of equals. Ones morals eat one's soul but that was accidental negligence. Moral degradation has had a place since.

The teenage brain

The teenage brain: A neuroscientists Survival Guide to Raising Adolescents and Young Adults.

I claim to be no expert except from my own experiences, I have no kids, this chapter was greatly inspired by the above.

The teen brain is not a fully developed brain this is at a very special point in development and growth. Stunning feats of learning are possible, but exuberance of adolescence not only bears fruit so quickly but prone to impulsivity, risk taking, irrational decisions, mood swings and poor judgement. We send adolescents mixed messages at this complex phase. Stay in their faces at this transitional time and keep them on the right path. Too much free reign is detrimental, have conversations and be patient and prepared. Changing their behaviour is your responsibility. This is done by remaining a good role model, advising and explaining. Parents can feel helpless but should take on responsibility for their teens irrational changes as they try to figure themselves out. Teenagers are often treated as adults, when the time between childhood and adulthood is tender.

Adolescence remains slippery. Teens are still working themselves out, made difficult by hormones that the brain is unfamiliar with. The teenage brain may feel the part but is highly underdeveloped with connections. This brain can signal dangers when a crisis arises, but the frontal lobe fails to respond to obvious ques. Talk to teens about the dangers of alcohol, give them case studies you have researched, there are hundreds of common horrific stories.

Teenagers' brains are the most vulnerable yet powerful, hence the irrationalism.

Alcohol can directly affect synapses in the brain and memory, the earlier in life and the bigger the binge of the alcohol consumption the damage can be more severe. Eccess alcohol causes brain cells to die. Think, is this worth a drink you probably won't remember.

Bias

The perceptions of the majority seem to lack the experiences of the minority. My books are reassuring people that don't have a platform to voice their views. We will have to repent in this generation not merely for the hateful words of the bad people but the appalling silence of the good people. Rev.Dr.Martin Luther King Junior. The Person you Mean to Be. Dolly Chugh.

We are not always the person we mean to be, I am not always who I mean to be. Most of civilization consider themselves to be a good person, all realities exist for different people, some of us are bias toward whatever minority you consider. Not only that but bias in ignorance totally believing we are correct. That is the meaning of bias, this is not intentional but harmful still. I am guilty of this, I have an example, I was shopping, at the cashier a woman in a wheelchair got to the conveyor behind me she had a basket on her lap and quite capably started putting her shopping on the belt, because she was in a wheelchair, I offered help to rightfully get snapped at NO! I would not offer to assist anyone else with their shopping and I quite comprehend why she seemed a little aggressive because I respond like this when people offer assistance for menial tasks. So even I am bias to exactly what I am campaigning for so can you comprehend how much of a battle we have.

Revolution needs heat (extreme movements, novelty) and light (entrance level protest, resolution) to have any affect. I am not a protest or rebellion familiar, but I have public spoken and published books all on my multiple causes: disability inequality, anti-drink/drug-driving, parenting, society, mind, I am as honest as my life realistically allows. I will not deny, I have admitted to my own unconscious bias, but I am conscious of some disturbing stigma thoughts, conscious but they appear unintentional because of my uncomfortable history with deeply psychological affect. I have grown much in my late thirties and more in the last six months since my very late maturing, have though developed totally identifiable identities that I am not proud of, these have to have little to no real world affects because they stay in my mind. Not refusing there is someone or somebody somewhere along that could know of these horrid thoughts. Once I quoted resistance is futile so my efforts to resist these by thinking no or the opposite, an advised method of counteracting negative thinking.

We can move from being good people to good-ish people and that is still okay, stay on track by feeling unease and guilt, shame is a tough one, I feel somewhat shameful but believe my lessons are tools for entering unfamiliar territory and a greater humanity.

Stereotypes have common features, competitive threat low warmth, a communal being is high warmth and competence, low status low competence and vice versa. High or low status affects groups, stereo types of black, homeless, drug addicts, people with disabilities are all low status, low groups are considered low status and low competence.

Psychological safety can mean we don't acknowledge our biases, growth mindset means we really look at ourselves, learn by taking risks and deepening superficial friendships. Wilful ignorance or wilful awareness. Nervousness and ignorance can be combatted by taking along a growth mindset.

We have another colossal task, just the words sex and gender is classed as unconscious bias, sex is biological gender is social, binary categories lead to more exclusion but all people are excluded from something or other so we should therefor all study becoming conscious of our invisible biases and become more aware of ourselves, this will lead to better humans and a better community the world over. If we think of people as high competence we think of them as individuals, low competence or status results in perceptual changes in visual acuity. Dehumanizing others in a non wholistic way is stereotyping. I do not want to fall into what is known as the warm glow affect and base my work on saviour mode or sympathy mode, these means I am not reciprocating and basing my work on my own needs. I disagree with D.Chugh, I have learned to tolerate my own needs to a small extent, and feel sympathy for minorities because I am in this group, I believe in my work and feel this to whatever extent may be considered saviour mode because surely will assist many different groups, from minorities experiencing prejudices and inequality to majority groups worldviews and unconscious biases encouraging and engaging in talking about issues that so many are biased about.

I as a white male have some ordinary privilege but as a disabled white male, I have a yet different privilege to women or blacks or the homeless or drug addicts or alcoholics. My best intentions are with this book and however you judge me just look at the messages, I am doing my bit to improve humanities dismay.

Anxiety

Did I cause my crash? Well yes in one sense, drink-driving is pretty conclusive, but my life has been and is leading to something even more affecting. This accident was a certain making of my adult life. Twenty years later after massive recouperation and delays I am finding heaven.

Anxiety is still with me but I battle through, I am a lucky one some find it impossible to live. Anxiety is a trapped place where often you envisage worst scenarios. This can lead to depression and extreme seclusion and behaviour.

Think of events that make you anxious, that interview or first date, now times this by 100 and try to consider those living with anxiety. Lonely not through choice but nerves and confidence. Beliefs are altered and we know by my other books the power of belief, this will adjust personality to fit. Some people, they are not rude just a casual meeting is beyond their comfort zone. Consider, I once was like this for various reason leading to anxiety, consider your comfort zone ending as you walk out the front door or even into the next room. We can have anxiety in a multiple of situations for many undecipherable explanations. Mine is difficult to apprehend so I try not talk about this but when the mystical enters your reasoning you are up against one large obstacle that many find incoherent to even discuss, so you bottle-up some more. Before you know it five years have passed and that now seems like a familiar different lifetime. You have changed much but still secretive. Professionals doing their best to withdraw you from yourself often step over the line of accepted questioning, which leads to defensiveness and disagreement. Although you cherish their efforts for help you wish they would not be so sneaky in their approach in investing revelation.

Anxiety minor or major is effecting to different degrees, if you have never lived with impairments of mental or physical kind this is hard explained as you will not totally accept and comprehend difficulties faced: watching telly, listening to radio, everyday conversations, eating and drinking, going outside, staying indoors, that exit, that shelf, that packaging, that colour, that car, with them wheels, with that number plate, with that bumper sticker, with that dent, in that place, that name, that design, that washing powder or washing up liquid, that toothpaste, that noise, that voice, that look, that shop, that road, that road sign, that turn, that roundabout, those traffic lights, them road works, travelling a certain direction, that number, that till, that clerk, with that badge, that shape and those letters etcetera etcetera etcetera etcetera. For me this includes most brands and things! So how do I live? Very, very difficultly but the lucky one is finding a way with minimal medication. You must ignore impulse, and that I hear is not healthy. I wash my clothes in plain water, don't brush, hardly eat or drink... but you wonder why I find comfort in weak beer... that I am not comfortable buying! and ignore my own instinct, that I hear is more not healthy. So, you could say I am ignoring healthy living, that I know is not healthy! Heaven help me, pleeease.

Life is King, this will teach however and whatever better than any other.

This enhances lives.

Email: your author.
drinkdrivedeterrents@protonmail.com
or
publicationjr@proton.me

Unapparent Nonsense Into Obvious Truth

I told my mother some of the trials people with disabilities face, she only started to acknowledge when she acutely started and continued observing those in my environment, wherever we were she witnessed the stares, the shifty eyes and looks of pity and disgust alike.

She really grasped these instances when she listened to other people's stories, also a personal experience when a passer gave her a look thinking she was drunk getting out her car, when she just has a balance and dizziness complaint. Or the people talking to her and getting all dismissive of me or having ridiculous expectation. She changed her attitude with what became obvious after learning. Families of those who suffer traumas will learn and evolve to very different than before an accident or illness.

Realities not observed are non-existent to the rest of the community unless they have complaints in their family. Even those who worked in a day centre for people with disabilities sometimes struggled to comprehend stories of an opposing society when told by delicate minds.

I totally comprehend why there are so many assumptions. Impaired people often have narrow views and thoughts, or conditioned reactions, this due to a force called society persuading them to recluse into themselves.

My threshold for keeping calm is crushed, often short tempered, contributions toward a taste of this are easy made. In a busy shop paying with Mum, she was scanning, I was bagging, she tried to pass everything to me instead of placing the item. Because I use my left side, she exaggerated smoothness of interaction, I could not grab hold of one item, so she twisted her wrist, back and forth and tilted the box. I shouted, swore and exclaimed just place them here. I lose my temper when people practice idiosyncrasies that are senseless to me.

I have heard people talking random words to themselves, even shouting, cognitively adjusted to resemble the figured by society, picture of either mental- health or a drunk. So can comply with why there are stigmas such as, ya do not approach these people, or be patient and give them time, which is often an over-the-top display that only contribute to more frustration.

The homeless have their own deviations, stigmas and opposition from the community. Therefore, homeless people and people with impairments can relate and do not judge so much. Homeless folk have been the one constant in my life, all the way through a severe disability.

Facts are true statements, unapparent nonsense are truths to a minority, they are however little apprehended as nonsense by the majority. Facts are truths, truths are ambiguous and hidden from one another but blatant to victims of uncertainties.

Do not judge others, because your truth is different from theirs, you might hold the true statement which is blatant unapparent nonsense to them. Not all people can know all truths or the nonsensical.

Obvious may seem, an assumption is never propositional learning. Feel yourself lucky to remain in an individual good place that in all considerations is not obvious truth, is more like unapparent nonsense, the click of a clock can determine how fast this good place alters, your world can turn upside down in the blink of an eye.

Make your way but incorporate others.

Identity and freedom of will

Identity is cultural and psychological, man forms him/herself when in groups, social order follows. He develops a self whether in solitude or not.

I will explain, I developed a persona that I started believing because I wrote every day, and on paper I was depicting sometimes my best sometimes my worst, again towards a purpose. I began forming a model. This was largely fictional, because I was guided by my literacy, was not until I found myself in interaction, I discovered my thinking was not accurate. I can think myself up a mountain when truthfully, I was nearing the gutter.

Also, I received Celestial guidance, suggestions kept arriving or I was transported by guidance found audiobooks, which some days seem to have stopped having inspirational content. Suggestion in thought was reciprocated by my writing.

Stimulation caused me bother as well, messages that appeared like a thought helps others think I am awakened, I am not... yet!

This got me considering my history, good and bad, had I been guided all this time? To get me into this requested place, requests not my own. I have heard that all I went through was necessary to get me here today. I ask again, is there really freedom of will when my thought has always been influenced?

I am sure there are those people who object immediately, I know fine that there is freedom just unsure as to contribution of acts. For example, the thought that led to action resulting in a feeling.

For a free world I feel rather constrained, by guidance, ego, and duty. I was guided to this arena of not feeling free, treated as correct area when I am continuing an intended route designed for a self that did not divert to the wrong. I always made things difficult for myself, but the achievements show determination.

Jim Rodriguez

I get enormous satisfaction from my work, one of very few things I get any satisfaction from. I know when I have something of value to others, am absolutely sure ya will gain, alteration in each who goes through my work.

Enjoy the learning.

Correspondence: Is Reality Real?

Humans have a variety of ways to represent structures of a world to themselves, thought, perception, beliefs, desires, picture and language. I will go through each individually and tell ya about my hard learned experience.

Thought; my thinking was limited when young, assuming I was great at everything, but I little appreciated my talents. Then brain-trauma, I lost my mental abilities and every item on this list. Stay the course and ya may gain gratitude at your own lives as I tell later how I rehabilitated to better than ever, only to have my mental capacity taken for a second time.

Inspired thought appears regularly as I tread through realities.

Perception: I was naïve until an adult, but my introduction to adulthood was disability, isolation, mental-health and an obscure community. When young I perceived everything was easy and that my life would go good. Must add, I received messages, that I then thought were just thought, messages that said all would evolve great.

I was never worried about the future, did not look very far ahead, lived for the moment. I started drunk driving, still did not think about a future; what if I crash? What will my life be like? How will my family change? These are all questions I did not think of until decades after a wreckage. A woman told me about her two sons, one was like me, living for the moment, the other thinks a lot way into his future, I bet he is a careful driver as he would have thought all the questions that take experience for me to think of.

Now I do lots of looking back which is taught as not healthy. Ya all looked back in my writing for a purpose. I also do lots of dreaming and planning about my amazing future. I write about my past, for a purpose, I also write the magnificent to encourage emergence.

Belief: my childish naïve beliefs of this being a harsh world full of deception and untrustworthy people I shame to admit, have returned after my thinking this is a beautiful place with many good people. Though there has been lies and deception even in Divine territories.

I have walked in more than one reality, some Divinely made, others catastrophe engineered.

My juvenile reckoning that disabled people are always moaning and always get better than equal treatment was a harsh one when I was forced to accept a truth. My beliefs are strongest in the efficiency of this material to attain more than one goal. My tragedies will teach, and friendships and families are livelihood determining I want this message heard. We can recover from anything when we make our own realities.

I also believed that only fools drank and drove and that I never would do such a thing. Let this subdue in your awareness, what ya think now may become entirely altered in ten years.

Desire: my wishes have changed since young, I have some, unrealistic to some in some worlds, desires but have desire about my place in a future more than I ever knew.

I have been to places desiring to have friends and been in a fantasy desiring to rewind time, not so I don't drink-drive but so I get my mistakes right, I had enlightenment knocking but failed to ascertain.

Statements- language, and what a person thinks- beliefs; presuppose to resemble what their reality is like, thus a model-picture, is formed of what they call home, my ordeals have meant acquisition of foreign territories.

Language: always one for communication and good conversation, until brain-damage meant word finding difficulties and temporary speech troubles.

Poem:

Heed

Creative brother.
Shadow withheld.
Scam a connection.
Ordinary unique.
Turmoil to report.
One place one cause.
Driven drunk.
Affects bilingual.
Ongoing centuries.
Author biographs.
Tricks in the temple.
Decipher abolish.

A place of no mercy, but is there such?

Greed and Fear

These are, to a large extent, how humans operate. Don't take offence, let me explain my rational:

They say not to do this, but our species wouldn't have survived if this was not factual, think of yourself first, greed. Or worry what others are thinking, fear.

In the company of a person with a disability, often people are wary, not sure of or think they have the person sussed, they tend to become overly nice or judgemental, the acceptable in between is less observed. Not to say this world is not full of purely pleasant people, these people, because of societal fear are fewer. By fear I also intend the psychosocial aspects of going with the crowd.

Not worrying what others are thinking is a healthy way to grow, ya can never satisfy everyone and living to your own honest values is recommended.

Although loneliness is one of the most common deficits, we live with this. A judgemental attitude will not even notice they are judging, a very lonely person who has lots of time to think in their own company, becomes very conscious, and I might say aware of social aptitudes. This lack of interaction interrupts the disfunction of the lonely person resulting in even more out of character displays.

Lonely people are trying to interact to the best of their ability, but this situation has them isolated, possibly they have social anxiety. Yes, there are those who prefer the quiet and their own company, but I would like nothing more than to build relationships of all kinds.

If even a minority feels confident in their argument, then they will speak up, but when they feel, their opinion will get objected by the group, they will likely keep silent. This is known as the spiral of silence. People may not realise or appreciate that maybe this person's life has already been destroyed and they only ruminate on mistreatment of any size.

The person in question may be vulnerable already only to feel more so, which may induce defensiveness and insecurity or less commonly, aggression. They cannot trust, possibly doubt everything therefore do not feel safe.

People may or may not be trying to intentionally hurt our emotions, but we sense invalidation, even when not there, we stop reaching out for emotional connection, so earn more of the exact reputation that we are trying to escape. This is frequently obsessed over.

Concepts

Your concept will remain different from mine, his/hers or theirs. As said, a successful world takes all kinds, each with their own worldview. We each look at different things with our individual perspectives. Some would sense a glass of water as half full, others would say half empty, a person stranded in a desert would water at the mouth and sense ultimate refreshment, a fish would wonder how the atmosphere can get put in a glass because it does not sense water as a separate entity, this is everywhere when they are at home.

Just like the place I have come to accept; the word disability is natural, and I don't hold inbred stigmas that I did when young. What is a disability and how does this affect people? There is no one answer to this question, just like no one person has the same fingerprint, no one person will have the same disability affecting in the same way. At a day centre for people after head-injury, yes, we all had the same trauma, affecting each to differing degrees and instances. Some had different physical problems, others had speech impairment, some of our memories were worse than others and so on. Even people with the same diagnosed disability, say autism, one name a myriad of different scales, effectors and with all people, disability or not, moods greatly enhance or detract the presentation of this person.

We all have thought and differing perspectives, affected by news, publicity, privacy, society- the group I spoke of earlier, and by what we hear and view. This will have astonishing impact, so partake a person with severe disability, possibly brain-damage affected their thoughts and views, doubly triggered by responding to the community warping out of shape when around them, perhaps stories of other people's disabilities affects them and gives them hope. We can all find discourse or desire in another's virtues, actions and speech. Or perhaps a poster remains in mind, so many different affecter's to so many differently affected.

So many differing portrayals of one subject, no wonder this is difficult to define and accept for some people. I am pleased to hear that children with disabilities are getting more fully integrated into mainstream schools. I have had many quiet years, not keeping up with current affairs, so much has changed so I apologise if I write how things were in my day but they are different now, I am still not fully clued into everything but I guarantee this book will educate, ya will learn something new. Is not an important quota if ya consider your educated enough, we all continue learning throughout life and all have something unique to teach.

Possibly ya think ya do not want to learn about us, just remember a lot of us were in your place of fitness once and possibly having the similar thoughts. Just consider the figures say with a high chance of occurring, that most people will, at some point in their life suffer from mental-health problems even physical disability, temporary or not.

Children in schools are the way forward, I can sense no alternative for what has been campaigned for years, exposure is a cure to most things, just as I say a parent will gain knowledge, acceptance, belief in horror stories of societies interaction with a child with a disability after living close by this child's experience. My Mum did not believe some of my stories until, after time, she began witnessing what I talked about.

Causal reasons are not enough for society, justify old age, accident, or illness, they are part of natural world, but never enough to cure the plight people with disabilities face every day.

Assumption is silly, some people assume I must have been born with a disability, or I was rebellious or must be trouble, but we all still say, do not assume anything: I never make assumptions.

I have attempted to justify why campaigners still struggle. What ya think is different from what he/she thinks, which is different again from what a child/adult assumes which is different from what a parent thinks. All of them are quite probably near opposite to what a disabled person knows. Why there is such a battle for inclusion.

Freewill or determinism, I say both are ruled out, if that's a possibility, before I reason my claim I say, if I have causal justification ya surely can understand a monumental battle, two opposite having been ruled out, there is a lot of ground in between. There is no such thing as totally freewill, some effects would affect. Say ya were presented with two entrances and ya must enter through one, but the one ya choose: freewill, is locked, so ya go through the other: determinism. Or something else, I got into the habit of examining number plates on cars, I swore they were delivery messages. Now I just do not look at anything that stimulates or causes discomfort, but the attention I focused my mind on became natural, so freewill of looking or not looking became routine to sense number plates, this is surely determinism, programmed after repetition. The mind taking the path of least resistance continues to divert attention, so I must adhere to what is determined, granted, by myself, and still look.

The natural world works on the path of least resistance, think of water travelling down a gully, this meander and wares a route that offers least resistance. As so for people, if resistance is detected survival mode kicks in and your more alert, the mind does not like risk which is then sensed. The mind cannot tell a difference between realities, imagined or not, and so, my hypothesis; disability discrimination, however interpreted on both sides, equals resistance, however undetected, resistance against obligation and regulation. People do not like to have their attitudes dictated, but the disabled person's imagination runs wild, reality creation! This may seem the reverse of what I intend but there is resistance on the disabled person view, resistance to get accepted, communicate, and live a regular life.

This then determines how ya unconsciously react, which makes most people uncomfortable. I am talking of my experiences long ago.

Reward is a monumental word for an operating mind, this goes out to all the scroungers that realise that vulnerability often leads to reward, gains of a certain nature, easily obtained, path of least resistance. Makes simple people like what they experience. Tell me no more, I do not need to learn of these people's morals.

This book has spanned many decades, information was correct at the time of writing.

Why have are there still drink-drivers and why do we have disability acceptance issues? Everyone I spoke to knows of people who have drink-drove, and some know of those who practice this regularly.

Disability issues, or a woman I got told to wobble off the other night, just because I was trying to make some friends. A woman said to me, oh things are a lot better now for disabled people, yes things are better than decades past but enter this world and your appreciation of neglect soars. Does this sound like a realm you'd like to enter? Watch what ya do then, devastation is very, very easily entertained.

Another issue; past influenced thought affects current thought which then goes on to comprehend my reality, leading to more influenced thought, which affects again, my reality is altered by so many repeating facets. All affecting my thought process which affected my world, and on and on. Why are we not taught in school of the power of thought and the Divine can affect every aspect of life, if you're doing things in secret, get real, somebody knows, and fate should not surprize if ya doing things that are ruled out.

Perhaps you're not living attempting to hide, whatever world ya live in, how'd ya get there? Partly luck, largely education, and largely the parenting ya received.

So, if a world is to progress, these need looking at, granted parenting or luck cannot be governed, but I am calling for an over hall to the education system. Emotional Intelligence, said more important than intelligence quota, should show in the curriculum. Catch up, this is the millennium.

Why Is Drink-Driving Still An Issue?

We all acknowledge we do not entertain thoughts of injuring ourselves or others, becoming disabled or even having an abrupt death, but do we really appreciate? Most of drink-drive offenders that I have acquainted were more concerned with punishment from courts and fines or driving bans. So, we can safely say that either way, there is no benefit or justification to drink-drive, we then ask so why do so many of us practice this?

Because this is so easy and convenient, but the saying, difficult roads lead to beautiful places is the same as easy things end in catastrophe and devastation!

Given the year and a promise of a leap in evolution, this is time to recognise hazardous pursuit we dare to endanger. Not only dangers considered, but wholistic self-worth will become each of our goals. Neglecting autonomy, because denying instincts or carrying on with immoral or unjust actions and attitudes is harmful and affecting to both giver and receiver, psychologically in major often unappreciated ways.

New habits will manifest, if the receiver continues to face prejudice and discrimination, survival instincts will take over his/her person. Thought, action and instinctual manner is now creating new neuronal pathways. The giver does not escape this affect, pathways will create that harden the undisclosed burden on the other. Cells shut down, reputations are formed, mind affects body so this will affect both giver and receiver health wise or other to different extents.

Once I was introduced, by a man who had studied brain, behaviour and human interaction, to the speculation that people's disabilities worsen, even physically because of how society relates to them. Since my study years I found more proof, this is science fact! Remembering my experiences, I can agree wholeheartedly.

After studying, I realized I have lived most my younger life in survival mode, this made for great astuteness and empathy, but when the opposition was the community, I had to re-survive in unaccustomed ways. Thoughts and attitudes that I always found ridicule with, I noticed I was having, even automatic, responsive facial expressions were surprising me. Every day was filled with new agendas I was forced to greet. This is the power of all our minds.

So, we can agree that a life with a disability is not our intention, but drinking, doing drugs, fighting, drink-driving or speeding are all a one- way ticket towards some form of disability/mental-health and eventually, premature death. Appreciate you cannot properly, a life of disability is very different to any realm of existence. Yes, all our realisms are different but unless you would like a totally abstract confusing view of social obscurity and your mind reaction of operating in survival mode full time and all our minds work in ways of least resistance, I would not act juvenile, rather spend twenty quid on a taxi, or arrive late, or give them a hug instead, and intoxicate yourself with love.

Look at prisoners in isolation, a massive affect is had on them. Any form of disability or difference from the norm can result in social solitude. A yearn to escape the silence just enhances neuronal fracturing. Is much like living as a prisoner in a world full of people, a deaf person in rupturing noise or a blind person in iconic beauty, there is no appreciation of another's abilities.

Social interaction is necessary for successful development in childhood and continues throughout life. Isolation is, I think a bigger cause of mortality and anguish than cigarettes, talk more on this later as this is fact.

We tend to shy away from strangers, this is advised to younger inhabitants and seemingly, due to disability/mental health, routine in a lot of adults. We are structured to pass our neighbours and community because we have somewhere to get, or I do not have time or patience. I am sorry to say, but those interactions of no personal gain are often sublimated. Partly why elderly people are so communicative, they may have experienced isolation and have certainly seen enough life to know you never know what you can learn from new acquaintances and there is always enough time just to acknowledge someone, whatever their stature. Also, older people know of the sense of nurture to the younger or impaired, but I must explain this view as well, they, stopping for a conversation, gain momentary relief from their possible silent loneliness, I think I talk of this later, all animalistic behaviours, including humans are ultimately selfish. This is natural how survival operates; we would never have survived if we did not consider self-first.

Society is vital for everyone, sure we get introverts, even they sometimes think there is something wrong with them, misfits are not introverts, they are more likely pushed out by an assuming community.

We are, a lot of us, anchored by oppression.

Humans operate in groups, how the group views the individual does also. Depending on status of looked at and viewer this is also true the other way, a person of high status might become mimicked by the whole group in varying ways. An expectation is that the individual will do as the group does, some seem reluctant to remain individual, why do ya think people of unique views are often held in high regard. The environment dictates to us all if we realise this or not.

There are many very caring people, we all admit to caring, differences in the same but few of us really look at ourselves and question our virtues and morals. If people really looked at what affects and changes their behaviours, they would have an insight into just how animalistic humans are. Example: The individual will most probably alter inbred attitudes when they witness the majority acting a certain way to say a minority. There's a famous saying about one person following the crowd.

Humanity

I have approached this writing in my unusual style, this is bereft with stages and jumps, I have left this so to portray my injury, not to gain sympathy but always my goal is to educate. Just witnessing my writing style and changes over the years offers a deferral for others to practice what brought me here. I have dreams that my writing will evolve humanity, I said that when I have the money, I will send a copy of these encyclopaedias to every school in the country but recently I had the wisdom of the audience the internet can offer. I shall restructure the globe and educate youth as too adults. I do not intend to boast but I have seen the power of my words, the lady on a drink-drive rehabilitation course whom I was introduced to as hard-core and beyond help, I saw her in town a week later, she proclaimed her gratitude for my talk and claimed never to drink-drive again, in fact she was trying to quit the alcohol. Or the school kids who were still talking about my talk the year after. Stay with me and I shall alter your beliefs.

This writing may seem interspersed and jumbled but the lessons are throughout, I have had a sublime, quiet, painful, hectic and emotional life, I always felt I was destined for greater things and my childhood, and that car crash were the making of my adult life.

Dreams of abolishing drink-driving, rejuvenating disability acceptance, promoting good living and soulful nurturing, because I am in a place that comprehends that we have a long way to go still to adjust to civilization in a proper form. Yes, there are those who feel objected, but these cannot truly accept disability equality or steep learning unless they are prone.

For I have studied hard, and learned so much, I shall teach inclusive the little-known neglects of society. We all can prosper and help each other to abundance. Each human deserves but there are us humans that have taken the grind and befell our goodwill and struggle to compensate.

I want this world to dance and rejoice in serving others, all can reclaim their birth rite of connection and bliss. The downtrodden are uplifted, the mighty are modest. Saints are some of these people but how do we know until we give them time?

The drink-driver who caused a wreckage is not appreciated, as human even! This is before certain prejudices are at play toward disabled people. One loses all his regard and distain becomes the forefront of his existence. You're not happy with life, and want difficulty, at every street and passage, the society cannot relate. That's ok, drink-drive then, thou will not have witnessed a world or community like this.

This podcast is the very small part of the start of a book, by similar title. I have much editing to do and have only just approached a publisher.

I will pause here with my view on just some things, as well as this book, that could, with much global benefit, get taught in schools, or at minimum attain public knowledge:

This Plan Is Apt

This plan is apt, for schools becoming proper foundations for youth. For this world to exhibit that which we are all capable, foundations must remain sturdy.

I propose lessons to include, cultural diversity including modules of micro aggressions: what these are and how they affect us and our neighbours.

My capable mind: The power of thought. Creating our reality.

Disability studies: Acceptance. Prejudice. Assumptions.

Until we meet again. With love.

Acceptance

Acceptance, this goes along with growing accustomed, which is where I stand out, I was never going to accept I was disabled, dark had shadowed my healthy life. I was told to rely on my wheelchair when I left hospital, except I got home, parked this in a corner and said that's the last time I get in that thing… and it was. I lurched everywhere at first, fell over lots, could not do stairs but I was convinced of my improvement. I still have a disability today but will not stop, twenty years of physical and mental recovery so I will not accept people treating me just like in the early days, I am striving for equal treatment.

I accepted in rehab that I would not sketch anymore or write with my dominant hand, I gave in finalising hand therapy, for a lazy take it easy guy I did work hard, results came quick and I had taken many shortcuts. Real dedication may mean there would be little physically wrong with me today, I use my impairments to deliver my messages. Hobbling back n forth in front of a hall of students is very prominent in delivering my anti drink-driving lesson.

I am very lucky.

Behaviours Are Reinforced

Behaviours are reinforced, a negative reaction will mean the behaviour is less likely to be repeated, a positive response means the behaviour is more likely to be repeated.

This is how we teach children but is just as true in adults.

Repetition and conditioning is how we learn and remember through behavioural psychology which is observable psychology, problem solving, remembering is cognitive psychology.

Person centred approach involves what is going on surrounding the person.

Communicate

The art of active listening, a lot of us take this for granted and think things like, oh, listening, that's easy, I have ears.

Have you ever been concentrating so hard on what you will say in response that you haven't been listening? Or interjected with what you were thinking when you have just been ask a question?

Yes, then you, like me can do good to practice active listening skills.

I chose to write about this subject because communication is a very important topic to me, one that has been abused my whole life.

People holding that you're the one with the issue not themselves or to go rambling on about something very important to you only to have the subject blatantly ignored and changed.

I have had my dignity crushed from those very things, I recognize, yet only display with very few people my honest value. So, very few people very few people communicate with me with any value, yes there have been times when this value went over my head and I just did not realize until later, if at all, which I can attribute to suffering brain damage years ago.

The accident, like for so many other people the physical problems resulting were not the most enduring. The emotional, communicative, and empathic kind were that.

My communication was temporarily affected so people found problems in simple communication with me, which many of them will not let go of.

Have you ever upset someone or shocked them years ago and they just cannot let the episode pass?

A side-affect from an accident, certainly for me is that we cannot always energize ourselves. Personally, I need a particular person with a very particular stimulating manner to do this for me. I have met many of these invigorating people, some in social spheres, some in professional ones but they all were passing moments, I have one of these people in my life currently, who promises me that we are not just having a moment, this is a lifetime friendship. Which is one of the most kind and important things anyone can say to another, is to me anyway.

But this was another lie. This very person went on tp abandon me after taking advantage. Yes, get this, she was a professional!

We cannot get to a deeper more intensive place in someone else from a shallow place within ourselves.

Our society is chock full of miscomprehension, we do not understand a lot of people but refuse to let this get known and carry on in our own blissful naiveties.

Memories

Memories, happy ones and thought-provoking ones.

Thought provoking:

The very first memory in my new life was in a side barred bed happily tracing lines on the ceiling, wondering how I got there. I thought I was out last night, I could still hear the laughs and club music, and taste tequila sunrise in that girl's kiss.

Had been 3 months, don't remember accident and emergency, I had a drunk-driving car crash! I was once in a-coma, 2points from brain death.

Back to surrealism, why are all my friends now in wheelchairs, and why do so many strangers enter my bedroom. Wait until I escape this matrix and find a phone box, mum will never comprehend this.

I thought the woman who visited me was an imposter, I thought I had everyone pretending to act as doctors and nurses sussed, their all in on this experiment, I know!

Then an angel walked in, what? I remember her from that life I dreamt!

No, this was real.

Spiritual Emphasis

This realism I was born into, does never deviate my true intentions anymore. Free will they say, when every major event in my life was encouraged by this influence.

Get real; if you're doing something ya shouldn't, someone/body somewhere knows, and the Universe can make an ultimate decision.

My evolution, I am arguing, was to train others, this day was always on an agenda. People I went to school with, names, events, even thought, was programmed by high forces and others, to conclude. Yeah, but ya misjudged me, nothing will sway my ambition to enhance humanity.

This life today is immersive in categories I cannot contain; most words resemble another meaning... in awakened life anyway. How do ya expect a book written or lessons spoken.

Life is unfair, just get on with what you've got, but ya so could make a best life. Remember that when things get tough.

Divinely orchestrated, I entered life and continued to grow in Heavenly lit occurrence. What I have to teach is a divinity, is not always Divine splendour.

Where I was born, who my parents are, my friends and acquaintances, the people I worked with, met and passed, and all the occurrence was untold prewritten, to teach, to strengthen. Yes, freedom of choice might have inferred directives of all these, but never once did I acknowledge a devious and cunning and spiteful holy people. Yes, I have had all these in different worlds. Sure they were explained to me once, but the lacking intelligent mind, due to such in question, intends I infer my interpretation.

Always when young, had thought life is going to get good, but also, inspired thought led me to daydreaming and imagining while in bed. Of disasters and of living a less lucky life... I had tremendous health issues, family troubles, social difficulties until I went overboard and had a drink-driving car crash... then in rehab, the psychologist miraculously altered my mind then removed such from my awareness.

For a good cause admittedly, he borrowed my mind to adjust this and I would have gotten back, if I made the right moves.

I was to go on and teach the world about the dangers of drink/drug driving. I did this anyway, including disability acceptance.

All without a mind.

Thing is, this was spiritually allowed, yes his delays, because they were earning, public sector money, for me to attend. And yes, he even accepted a brain-damaged opinion of, oh I don't need a psychiatrist, they're for mad people... I am not on a lot of medication, psychologists like to do their work without medication.

Rehab, in all their games, lost a video of my very impaired walking before my recovery.

Instilled recurring thought from people throughout my life and psychologist, were divinely remembered to assist, to hinder, to deviate and direct, but some of the babble I was told, was not by experts. Do they not know how powerful a subconscious mind is? Not knowing what to do, when gone times I was told what I should do, what I should not do, and what I would probably do that was not advised. Put a blurb in someone's head, they will likely recall the negative first and go with any memory they have. Doh, they should have only told me what I should do.

Thought became speech or rather speech became thought, rhymes became dictated to appease colours, numbers, letters, objects, patterns, designs. All of which I divinely discovered in research or even when looking at posters.

I cannot accustom or even write all the deviances of a so-called awakened world, but my expectation and thought created a reality full.

Careful what ya imagine, think, speak or write.

Spirituality I don't want to accuse, but something was clawing at my soul, my work, and my abundance. So whatever/whoever can walk on, I am over in believing in your victory, I am the victorious because the Universe and Angels know my true intention, and this was Spirituality that made a difficult path add to difficulty.

So, where respect is due, I give my gratitude, but most we are taught is faff.

Have faith in yourselves and nothing, not the mightiest can defeat ya.

Evoked by those that know! Yes, a spiritual world made a bodge. Awakened people years ago, told me names and instances, then told me to forget everything. I have written about subconscious mind power and that this recalls everything, and negatives are likely recalled prior to anything else.

Those that think I am awakened are mistaken, these memories haunt, how else do I know stuff, names included, to coincide with a thought that I was told not to have. Names that are very, very commonly utilised words. How does a person write, speak, think or listen to music without incorporating these very, very regular words?

Bodge!!!

Happy times:

I miss a lady I used to go out with, kind of, was unofficial but we sat and laughed all the time. She'd have to wait for a stuttered, giggling punchline.

We never watched telly, we communicated always. Bedroom life was ecstatic! 😌

Did not realize then, not until months after letting her slip by going away to rehab, did I realize, I loved that woman! Only love of my life and I didn't comprehend what love does.

Lyn thankya, these memories have helped me through tough times, I shall never forget ya. Kisskis.

A land no one knew:

Once upon a time, in a land far far away… but in this world… or on this planet rather, because this was not in these worlds!

Was an abstract place, with hidden decimal points guiding, fakedly obviously as necessity to a path for civilization in any kind of regularity.

Celestial light is with everyone, all my life but this shone brightest after my learning to respect very little, I did some, out of character… but then no one, not even me knew my true character, out of character actions. I was educated in a facade, to grow more facade!

I talk much more about Divinity throughout.

Joys of a difficult but fantasy childhood, were awash with lack when I collided with self responsibility, yes I was curteous but this was intimidation, later years reveal, with facade remember so even my family were unnaware. There was a lot of self deceit and fronts posed.

Very intelligent in mind I managed to have similar but very different relations to all. Now middle aged, I have resided in almost as many residences as years of life. Built one character in school, had to alter when relocation meant different school. Have one character in a city, needs must alter dramatically when residence is suddenly a sleepy country village.

Family, health, study, work, play, drink, drugs, residential work, vehicles, social life, accidents, fights, crime... All contradicted what I presented to my family, but they were happy plodding on thinking they did an excellent job. They did in most regards, just wholistic character building and self worth were a myth to them.

I try and give credit where due, they each had they're own difficulty growing up. So this really does pass down from generation to generation. They say, and I know, that a parents invisible beliefs or secrets, a child intuitively senses and learns from unnaware to themselves or probably even both parents.

Like I grew thinking one parent was a saint because they were always right, so they like to think. I get emails from many people who are aware, shall we say. Many say occurences weren't my fault, this persons says why believe an email more than anyone else?

Considering this person is a medium and senses a lot of things, she is miffed by childhood neglect, centuries of oposition with an elder in my household, loneliness, lost roots, health, and the significance of their whimsy approach to a skilled job of parenting and childhood development into teenage and adolescence.

People may acknowledge some bitterness here, they are right, just wait to regard life when I speak of other atrocities, of family, friends, aquaintances, neighbours, passing community, and yes a bulk of this is Spiritual.

Even Divinity misled me!

Dead real:

What do you think about Spirituality? Compassion, kindness.

My world was shaken, then revolved! Yes I admit, partly due to my failure, at astrolical magnitudes. Yes if I had adhered to every required attribute, this could have been easier, but that is why I refer to my foundations. If I was known to hold such promise, and I was, because aware people hinted at, then abstract intricusies my whole life. Why was I not presented life such like The Dalai Lama? Who met and left his parents to go with an utter stranger! Because he felt his purpose. And why did I acquaint every challenge of the awakened few, and strict life determining incidents?

I can answer that question!

I always felt I was meant for more than this unlucky mediocre life, I started one purpose, write books, make podcasts and public speak. This has evolved into what you're looking at. I quote myself: Always knew I would potentialy affect divine evolution of this planet.

Spirituality, is not what you think, this has many many dualities. Depending on the statures of the initiative, all ecquates to what is prescribed. I knows Mediums who struggle with my decription of life and reality, they attribute everything I say to mental health!

Mental health started me rhyming word, but Spirituality along with my dismissive education got me on this path. I rhyme red with dead, what do ya know, rhyming or rather using a first letter, of a storename d-something town, with deadtown, Heaven decended, but there are other dead entities too. This town, the people, places, building munch (my term for food, because foo or vu is Voo-Doo). All began to frequent that town!

Are ya started to comprehend, how honoured I am they thought I just might remain strong enough to not only live brain-damage, major disability, social ostricysation, health issues, mental-health issues, but retain ability to teach and produce?

Also every sylable or number resembles something else to me, because I have memory, or guided thought/inspired thought, of these awakened individuals telling me stuff!...

Don't go but take everything.

Don't sink or swim.

Don't eat damn eat. -(don't eat the meat).

Don't ever say ever, never, robert, william, matthew etc, you, to, use, words, word, it, I, them, the, awaken, tree, lucy, table, bell, church, see, or anything that ends in a multiple of letters, which in language there are millions! Oh there is a million more but my damaged brain doesn't always operate when duty calls.

And I can write, oh yeah theres another, right/write! Teach and educate, admittedly-and another! Admittedly I have forgotton most my phenominal experiences and I have to use these word at one time or another, but you still may want to call me a lier at the end... Don't, I am just assisting people to regard life and consider difficulty, if difficulty really presents.

I opposed some regulation, so when I did eat dam eat, this was gricille of dead! I know ya have difficulty apprehending, but enter a world where anything is possible. Physics says that even a rock is not solid, it's just that rock atoms move slower, I have witnessed whole building shift perspective from one side of a carpark to another. I have witnessed vast meadows appear down what was a narrow town cobbled street. I have walked in copices absolutely ground covered in four leaf clovers.

Adhere to signs:

I was told don't look but notice everything, I was meant to know when I was getting a sign and do what this suggested. I was told to stop eating and told not to go in any extablishment until a new world, I went in practically every place in town!

Later realisation tells me, I did not do pretty much most what I was meant, that was until the new world emerges, a secret solstice not everyone knows of, then or now I must do everything opposite of which way I did. So, went everywhere – now nowhere to go. Ate lots and little- now dont eat, only made half day so far, I used to go 3-4 days on two sandwiches, this must be possible, Jesus went on a fast for 60 days, I haven't even done three days yets, but whats one of the important things we learn? Ya must eat, ya got to nurish.

Don't go to the station, so I fretted when I did, but they actually meant petrol station, don't buy the flamable liquid, they meant alcohol from a petrol station. Don't go there on this day, did. One person, bearing in mind at one point I was meant to copy these people picked a beer right in front of me, I thought no! So I bought munch, this was constrained to things I should not eat, something reputed to keep ya awake or have nightmares. We'd just spoken about doing stuff on a certain day and what this intends.

Some nights I had insomnia, could not sleep, I am more carefree when lacking sleep, so I went and I bought, I ate some. I was so tired went bed at 5pm, slept 3hours- but the worst nightmare and sweats! Now I am scared to sleep, doing things on that day an old wives tale is, you'll do them everyday rest of year. So I am not expecting much sleep so I started writing.

A new world:

I was to create this new world! With mental health after Spirituality totally removes my mind from my awareness. Yes I reside in a, later recalled, place I should only go to when I suceeded at other missions. Accuse somebody else not me if this world is bad.

How is a civvy, with no foundations or learning supposed to reconise all the subtle gestres of an invisible world. They knew I'd fail, but they still let me continue. Where there is no life respect in Spirituality, there is no world!

A new perspective, my life experience was and is meant how this is, to teach others: power we all own, to construct our own realities, power of thought, intention and belief.

I construct the perfect reality where all communicate and like each other, with deviance, crime, cruelty, secrets and lack abolished.

Remember This

This work was, in a way, compulsory, because I knew I was to get back to fitness, I worked hard and kept searching.

So, if ya don't envisage doing half the work that led to this book, ya know what not to do. Drink-driving is easy, and the consequences are not.

Yes, easy, convenient, fast, the same goes for you're deterioration in ability, mental prowess, relationships, skills and everything that makes ya a regular human.

Ya will never have bigger regrets, firstly, I knew I should not so why did I do that? Then ya remember viewing parts of my story, and kick yourself for not taking note.

I don't know your lives, same as ya don't realize what I have been through these twenty odd years. So, are we at a mutual place? From my heart, I am confident in saying, respect lives, don't drink/drug drive or speed, or get a conscience for the people ya injured, or go to prison charged with murder for the people ya killed, or live in lonely isolation colliding with society with your disability.

If ya insist you're invincible, then save others the heartache and choose the headstone for your very own grave.

I know the advice is to finish books on a happier note than the previous, so here this is;

Implanting Lessons

Implanting lessons is my intention.

I had difficulty throughout life, until the accident, then I accepted what proper difficulty was!

Ignored all the scrapes and near misses in my car, was even pulled over and breathalysed by police… the week after I was in a drunk-drive car crash! Accident and emergency for two months, unconscious for six weeks, in a coma two points from brain-death, hospital for another three months. My reality was shaken, I did not know who my family were, I thought friends were angels from that life I dreamt, thought I was out the night before but this was four months later.

Was in a wheelchair to start, could not do stairs, uneven ground or grass even, could not integrate and socialise, could not eat without choking, could not communicate, brain-damage meant real word finding trouble and a massive stutter. I have a tear as I write this.

They thought I would not manage on my own, I moved into my own place a year after home from hospital. Day centres, hospitals and mental-health units, doctors were most of the next few years. Ten of them, relocating after my neurology caused issues with the community- in every town.

I finally settled after much relocating in a town, there has been over twenty years of disability, mental-health, relationship troubles, very few friends and societal collision.

Been through much but am kind of happier now, I am very lucky. Onwards to great things, I am still hopeful, use my story to learn by because I can tell ya, a lot of people would not have had the determinism and belief to get this far.

Thankya for staying the journey, and please, do yourself and everyone a favour, try not drink/drug drive or speed, suicide is just as good.

After saying I would help by not ending on a sad note, I AM ALIVE AND DOING GOOD.

Love to ya all, your author.

To Our Future

Doing things back to front or an in an inversed procedure I say, results in a greater wisdom: My battles with drink, loneliness, medication and deluded thought, has taken over 30 years of suspicion, doubt, questions and near loss of faith, actually thats not true, I knew always deep within my mind this was all for a purpose. Have sustained an unshakable inner knowing and outer surrender to seclude part of a journey we call life.

Let me tell you, highs and not so, friendship and isolation, social and residential, from young to middle aged, inspired thought gifted supremity and destruction that all led to continued wisdom and learnt agendas. Suicide pivotals are one sign of near defeat that I was supposed to live through to grant an appreciation for minor or major attributes, in ecquistic subtleties in array.

I had to experience lows and depressions before ecstasy began in small increments but this is after only 12th day of not drinking!

Is now very apparent to me that alcohol was keeping me trapped, others said thats your mental health made worse by the alcohol, after thinking a confused Divinity was ushering my reality, I am starting to agree. Although I am also starting to think, Divinity was not confused, I was!

Saints tried to rescue me from losing a Divine existence, but I continued drinking to expose a plain reality. This will still evolve to sublimacy of different appeasements, afterall I have learned so much that the drink was obscuring from me, now un-intoxicated I can ponder and contemplate, perhaps just that will create what I was, in denial, so much striving for. Added lessons of which I have suffered multiple are content for writing.

Mentioned isolation, I have started to socialise a bit, and find awkwardness in really connecting because I am or was so in a routine of only practicing this when drunk, I am unnaclimatised to sober interactions I must ecquate back to normality. One of many classes that taught me have me comforted in knowing that the more I do this the less uncomfort will present.

To our future

Still Have Faith

I feel that I obscured myself, or rather the alcohol kept things from me, fourteen days without and this is all appearing suddenly.

Do not like a fact I said some of the things I did, I curate new adgendas.

When I was a child I believed in a fantasy about this life, let me tell ya all, those fantasies are reality. By your speech and thought, believe and think, ya surely view in a mirror of life. People, places, structures and all, I can say, I should know the rewards of not doing so, don't hold grudges or resentments.

Make every laugh and good time a remembered miracle. Find or remember Love in everyone, have no fear.

Erase sorrow and fear.

My top recommendation:

If ya look at nothing by Jim, listen to this: Live in Harmony with the Universe - Metaphysics for Everyone - Conny Mendez - AUDIOBOOK

Our evolution.

Bibliography

Avoiding conflict does not usually lead to peace, M.L. Owens, S.R. Banks, L D. Anderson.

Behaviour In Public Places, Erving Goffman.

Friendship. The Evolution, Biology and Extraordinary Power of Life's Fundamental Bond., Lydia Denworth.

Healing The Fragmented Selves of Trauma Survivors, Janina Fisher.

How To Talk So Kids Will Listen. And Listen So Kids Will Talk, Adele Faber and Elaine Mazlish.

Learn Faster and Better, Josh Eyler.

New Frontiers In Mirror Neurons Research, Pier Francesco Ferrari, Giacomo Rizolatti.

Recovery and Mental Health, David Pilgrim and Thomas Luckman.

Sway, Pragya Agarwal.

The Book You Wish Your Parents Had Read (And Your Children Will Be Glad That You Did), Philippa Perry.

The Construction of Social Reality, John R Searle.

The Seat of the Soul, Gary Zukav.

The Social Construction of Reality, Peter L Berger and Thomas Luckman.

Live in Harmony with the Universe. Metaphysics for Everyone, Audiobook, Conny Mendez.

Email: your author:

drinkdrivedeterrents@protonmail.com

or

publicationjr@proton.me

This book is available worldwide from Amazon and all good bookstores

Michael Terence Publishing
www.mtp.agency

www.facebook.com/mtp.agency

@mtp_agency

www.ingramcontent.com/pod-product-compliance
Lightning Source LLC
LaVergne TN
LVHW041647060526
838200LV00040B/1745